Green Smoothie Revolution

The Ultimate Guide to Delicious and Nutrient-Packed Smoothie Recipes for Optimal Health and Craving Satisfaction

MENDOCINO BROCK

3

Table of Content

Mendocino Brock

Book Introduction:

Welcome to The Ultimate Smoothie Recipe Book: Experience the Power of Green Smoothies with Nutritious and Tasty Recipes. This comprehensive guide aims to not only satisfy your cravings with nutritious, delicious smoothie recipes but also be your one-stop book for creating delicious and nutrient-packed smoothies for every taste and occasion.

From the refreshing coolness of a green smoothie to the energizing blend of a breakfast shake, the world of smoothies is both expansive and wonderful. This book offers you an introduction to this universe, one filled with taste, health, and versatility. The recipes contained herein offer a comprehensive guide to creating the most nutritious, delicious, and innovative smoothies. Whether you're a novice, experienced smoothie enthusiast, or a health-conscious individual, there is something for everyone in this book.

Smoothies have long been appreciated for their convenience and health benefits. The ease of packing nutrients into a single glass, the simplicity of the process, and the delightful taste all make them an ideal choice for those looking to maintain a healthy lifestyle in our fast-paced modern world.

This book is designed with a holistic approach to health and nutrition. The variety of recipes included caters to diverse dietary needs, from vegan to gluten-free, while focusing on taste, nutritional value, and health benefits. Each chapter is dedicated to a specific category of smoothies, making it easier for you to navigate based on your personal preferences and needs.

The book starts by explaining the power of green smoothies, offering a solid foundation of understanding before you dive into the recipes. As you navigate through the book, you'll discover smoothies tailored for different occasions and needs, such as energizing breakfast smoothies, post-workout recovery blends, savory smoothies for dinner, and even dessert smoothies that won't ruin your diet.

Beyond these, the book explores antioxidant-rich and superfood smoothies, a range of detoxifying blends, and immunity-boosting concoctions. There's a special chapter dedicated to kids, ensuring that even the pickiest of eaters can find a smoothie to love. In addition, this book acknowledges the dietary needs of those following vegan, keto, and gluten-free diets, ensuring that everyone can enjoy the wonderful world of smoothies.

Finally, the book concludes with a chapter on the art of smoothie-making. After all, a smoothie is more than the sum of its parts. By following the provided tips and tricks, you'll be able to craft the perfect blend each time, making your smoothie journey as smooth as the drinks themselves.

Chapter 1

The Power of Green: The Basics of Green Smoothies

Welcome to the world of green smoothies! As one of the most powerful tools in the healthy living toolbox, green smoothies have earned their place in the hearts of fitness enthusiasts, health gurus, and people seeking a more nutritious lifestyle all over the world. These smoothies are a clever way to pack in a ton of essential nutrients into a single meal or snack. The idea is simple – combine leafy green vegetables with delicious fruits and blend until smooth. The result is a delicious, nutrient-dense beverage that's as good for your health as it is for your taste buds.

The key to a great green smoothie lies in striking a balance between your fruits and vegetables. A good rule of thumb is to aim for about 40% greens to 60% fruits, but this can be adjusted to your taste. The fruits bring the sweetness and mask any bitterness from the greens, making these smoothies a great way to sneak extra vegetables into your diet, or the diet of a picky eater in your family. Leafy green vegetables are nutritional powerhouses packed with vitamins like A, C, K, and many B vitamins, as well as minerals like iron, calcium, and potassium. They also contain dietary fiber, which aids digestion and contributes to a feeling of fullness, making green smoothies an excellent tool for weight management. Not to mention, the phytonutrients found in leafy greens have been linked to a reduced risk of chronic diseases, including heart disease and cancer.

Different greens bring different nutritional profiles to the table. For instance, kale is known for its impressive vitamin A and C content and is a good plant-based source of calcium. Spinach is particularly high in iron and magnesium. Swiss chard stands out for its unique phytonutrient profile, including syringic acid and kaempferol, which have powerful health-promoting properties. Therefore, it's a good idea to rotate your greens to ensure you're reaping the benefits of a variety of nutrients.

Fruits, on the other hand, add more than just sweetness to your green smoothie. They're also loaded with essential vitamins, minerals, and antioxidants that can enhance your health. For instance, berries are packed with antioxidants that fight inflammation and help protect your cells from damage. Citrus fruits are rich in vitamin C, which supports immune health, while bananas provide a good dose of potassium, an essential mineral for heart health.

In addition to fruits and vegetables, there are several other ingredients you can add to your green smoothie for an extra nutritional punch, including protein sources (like Greek yogurt, tofu, or protein powder), healthy fats (like avocado, flaxseeds, or chia seeds), and liquid bases (like water, almond milk, or coconut water). These recipes are just a starting point for your green smoothie journey. As you become more comfortable with these combinations, I encourage you to start experimenting with your own. Remember the basics: a good balance of greens and fruits, a source of protein if it's serving as a meal replacement, and a healthy fat to ensure you're absorbing all those fat-soluble vitamins in your veggies.

One of the most wonderful things about green smoothies is their versatility. You can adjust them to meet your dietary needs, taste preferences, and even your nutritional requirements for the day. Had a heavy lunch? Opt for a lighter smoothie with plenty of greens and a light base like green tea or coconut water. Need a post-workout pick-me-up? Add some Greek yogurt or a scoop of protein powder for muscle recovery. The possibilities are endless. Another great aspect of green smoothies is that they can be enjoyed at any time of the day. While they're traditionally known as a breakfast staple, there's no wrong time to enjoy a green smoothie. They can serve as a quick and convenient lunch, a mid-afternoon energy boost, or a light dinner option. Plus, they're portable, making them a great option for those busy days when you're on the go.

A final word on the power of green smoothies pertains to their benefits beyond physical health. Sure, they're great for your body, providing essential nutrients and promoting optimal health. But they're also beneficial for your mental wellness. A diet rich in fruits and vegetables has been linked to improved mental well-being, including reduced symptoms of depression and anxiety. This mental health boost is just another reason to make green smoothies a regular part of your lifestyle.

Superfoods like spirulina, an algae rich in protein and vitamins, can greatly enhance the value of your green smoothies. Chia seeds or flaxseeds offer a boost of healthy fats and fiber. Don't forget about goji berries, a powerhouse of antioxidants, or matcha powder, a form of powdered green tea that provides a host of health benefits from improved brain function to cancer-fighting properties. Smoothies can be customized in numerous ways to suit your dietary needs and taste preferences as well. Want a protein kick? Add a scoop of protein powder or a dollop of Greek yogurt. Want a creamier texture? Blend in some avocado or a spoonful of nut butter. Need a touch of sweetness? A bit of honey or a few dates can do the trick. Looking for more flavor? Add a pinch of cinnamon or a splash of vanilla extract. The possibilities are endless!

The key to manipulating your smoothie's texture lies in the balance of your ingredients. For a thicker smoothie, add more frozen fruits or veggies or a handful of oats or chia seeds. For a thinner smoothie, simply add more liquid base. If you want to enjoy your smoothie later or prepare several batches for the week, knowing how to properly store them is crucial. While smoothies are best consumed immediately after preparation, they can be kept in the fridge for up to 24 hours without losing too much nutritional value. Be sure to store your smoothie in an airtight container, and give it a good shake or stir before consuming as separation is natural.

Making green smoothies a part of your regular diet can seem daunting at first, especially if you're new to the world of leafy greens and superfoods. Here are a few tips to help ease the transition: start with mild greens like spinach before moving on to more bitter ones like kale or dandelion greens; balance the greens with sweet fruits to make the taste more palatable; and experiment with different combinations to find what you enjoy.

The reason why green smoothies have gained immense popularity in the health and wellness realm is largely due to their plethora of health benefits. They are filled with fiber, which aids in digestion and keeps you feeling satiated, helping in weight management. The antioxidants present in these smoothies combat inflammation, while the wide array of vitamins and minerals support overall health and vitality. Green smoothies are also a great way to boost your daily vegetable intake, especially for those who struggle with consuming enough greens.

As with any trend in the health and wellness world, there are several myths surrounding green smoothies. One such myth is that they're too high in sugar. While it's true that fruits contain sugar, they're also loaded with essential vitamins and fiber. The fiber slows down the absorption of sugar into your bloodstream, preventing the spikes in blood sugar that you'd get from consuming refined sugars. Another myth is that the fiber in smoothies is destroyed during the blending process. While blending does break down the fiber, it doesn't eliminate it. In fact, blended fruits and vegetables can sometimes be easier for your body to digest.

To create a delicious and healthy green smoothie, there are a few common mistakes to avoid. One of these is not including enough protein. If you're drinking a smoothie as a meal replacement, it's important to add a protein source like Greek yogurt or a scoop of protein powder to make it more balanced and filling. Another mistake is not rotating your greens. Consuming a variety of leafy greens ensures that you're getting a wide range of nutrients and also helps prevent you from building up a high level of alkaloids, compounds that can cause mild symptoms if consumed in large quantities over time. The blender you choose can have a big impact on the texture of your smoothie as well. High-speed blenders are capable of pulverizing even the toughest ingredients, resulting in a smooth and creamy smoothie. However, if you're on a budget, a regular blender can also get the job done. You may just need to blend your ingredients in stages to ensure everything is evenly processed.

Green smoothies are versatile and easy to incorporate into your daily routine. You can enjoy them for breakfast, as a snack, or even as a meal replacement. Some people find it helpful to prepare their smoothie ingredients in advance and store them in the fridge or freezer to make assembly easy. If you have picky eaters in your household, green smoothies can be a great way to sneak more veggies into their diet. Start with sweeter fruits and gradually increase the amount of greens as their palate adjusts. You can also try fun and creative presentations, like serving the smoothie with a colorful straw or topping it with a bit of granola or some fruit slices.

By now, you should be well-equipped with the basic knowledge of green smoothies – from their nutritional benefits to their versatility in meeting various dietary needs. As we journey further into this book, you'll explore more about specific recipes, additional superfoods to enhance your smoothies, and even how to use smoothies as part of a cleanse or detox program. So grab your blender and your favorite leafy greens and fruits, and let's continue this exciting journey to health and wellness together. You're ready to unleash the full power of green smoothies!

As we wrap up this comprehensive introduction to the world of green smoothies, remember that this is just the beginning. The journey to good health and tasty food doesn't end here. As we go forward, we will explore new, exciting recipes and dig deeper into the world of nutritious, tasty, and fulfilling smoothies. You now know why green smoothies are popular - their health benefits are as vast as the array of ingredients you can use to make them. You've also learned how to avoid common pitfalls when making your smoothies, and how to adjust the consistency to suit your preference. You've discovered that with the right blend of ingredients, green smoothies can help support weight loss, enhance digestion, and boost your intake of fruits and vegetables. You've even learned how to make green smoothies appealing to the younger members of your family. Your journey to understanding the power of green is well underway.

As we dive into morning smoothie recipes, remember that smoothies are extremely customizable to suit your personal tastes and health goals. Don't be afraid to experiment with different ingredients and tweak recipes to your liking. A morning smoothie should energize you while providing balanced nutrition to power you through the day.

Let's start with some classic fruit-based smoothies. The Sunrise Strawberry Banana Smoothie combines protein-rich Greek yogurt, oats, strawberries, and banana for a meal-like beverage. The oats add fiber to keep you full and focused. Strawberries are packed with vitamin C to support immunity, while banana provides potassium for heart health. For a tropical twist, try a Pineapple Coconut Smoothie using coconut milk as the base and accenting it with lime juice. The healthy fats in coconut milk promote satiety and balance blood sugar, while the pineapple and lime provide a dose of vitamin C.

Moving on to green smoothies, the Morning Green Revitalizer Smoothie packs a nutritional punch with spinach, banana, pineapple, coconut water, and chia seeds. Spinach is rich in carotenoids, vitamin K, and folate. Pineapple and banana provide fiber and potassium. Chia seeds add protein, fiber, and omega-3 fatty acids to keep you fueled till lunchtime. If you need an extra nutrient boost, add your favorite greens like kale or Swiss chard along with superfoods like spirulina or maca powder.

Looking for a vegan protein kick? Try a Peanut Butter Banana Smoothie made with pea protein powder, almond milk, peanut butter, and banana. You get muscle-building protein, healthy fats from the peanut butter, potassium from the banana, and vitamin D and calcium from the fortified milk. Dates can be added to enhance the sweetness too. For a lower calorie option, replace the peanut butter with a tablespoon of ground flax or chia seeds.

If you need help with digestion, a Green Apple Smoothie with spinach, green apple, parsley, lemon, ginger, and water makes for a refreshing morning beverage. The greens provide fiber, while the lemon adds electrolytes and the ginger aids digestion. The juices in the green apple and lemon can also help alkalize the body. Digestive enzymes or probiotics can be stirred in as well for an extra gut health boost.

Now let's talk coffee smoothies for those who need their morning caffeine fix. An iced Coffee Banana Smoothie is perfect for summer with cold brew coffee or espresso, milk of your choice, banana, ice, maple syrup, and a dash of cinnamon. The banana provides potassium to balance the acidity from the coffee, and the cinnamon adds an extra punch of antioxidants. For a mocha version, add cocoa powder or chocolate protein powder.

If you prefer hot coffee smoothies, try blending your hot coffee with milk, cocoa powder, banana, peanut butter, and ice for a Frosty Mocha Smoothie. The peanut butter and banana lend creaminess, and the cacao provides stimulative theobromine in addition to caffeine for an energizing sip. For a lower calorie option, replace the peanut butter with a tablespoon of ground flax or chia seeds.

Let's segue into some green tea smoothies, which provide the alertness of caffeine plus the health benefits of antioxidants like EGCG. A Matcha Green Tea Smoothie is soothing yet energizing with blended matcha powder, banana, spinach, and almond milk. Antioxidant-rich matcha may boost metabolism and focus without the coffee jitters. For black tea instead of green, an Earl Grey Smoothie with black tea, banana, Greek yogurt, and lemon makes for an elegant breakfast sip.

We can't talk morning smoothies without mentioning protein-rich yogurt smoothies. A Mango Coconut Yogurt Smoothie blends coconut yogurt with mango, coconut water, chia seeds, and lime. The protein in the yogurt combined with fiber from the chia keeps you satiated, while the coconut water replenishes electrolytes lost during sleep. For a nutritious post-workout recovery drink, whip up a Cherry Vanilla Smoothie with cherry juice, vanilla yogurt, banana, and ground flaxseed. The yogurt provides muscle-nourishing protein while the flaxseed aids in muscle repair.

While fruit and veggie smoothies are great, don't forget about the inclusion of healthy fats to balance blood sugar, provide satiety, and aid nutrient absorption. An Almond Butter Smoothie is a filling option with almond butter, banana, cinnamon, maple syrup, milk, ice, and shredded coconut on top. Or try an Avocado Coconut Smoothie using avocado instead of nut butters as the healthy fat source. The avocado lends a rich, creamy texture.

If you have a nut allergy or prefer to avoid nuts, sunflower seed butter or pumpkin seed butter make great replacements in smoothies. Hemp seeds and chia seeds also work well as plant-based sources of omega-3 fats and protein. Additionally, tahini made from sesame seeds adds a toasty, nutty flavor to smoothies. Ground flax and chia can even be used to create "eggs" in vegan smoothies for added protein.

Preparing smoothie ingredients in advance saves time in the morning rush. Wash and chop fruits and veggies on the weekend, then store them in sealed containers in the fridge for up to 5 days. You can also batch blend smoothies and refrigerate for up to 48 hours. Or try freezing pre-portioned smoothie packs in reusable pouches to create grab-and-go morning meals.

While classic blender smoothies are convenient, don't limit yourself to drinkable smoothies. For days you have more time, explore the world of smoothie bowls. These thick, spoonable smoothies make for a fun breakfast presentation while providing balanced nutrition. Start with a base of blended bananas, mangos, pineapples, or other fruits. Then layer your toppings like granola, nuts, seeds, coconut flakes, cacao nibs, peanut butter, and berries. You can even make a green smoothie bowl using spinach or kale as the base.

Smoothies are also a great way to use up ripe produce before it goes bad. Overripe bananas lend sweetness, while spotty berries pack concentrated flavor. You can even rescue veggies on their last legs, like spinach or kale, by blending them into nutrient-dense smoothies. Just be sure to examine your ingredients and remove any moldy or rotten bits before adding to your blender. Putting food waste to use in smoothies is rewarding both for your wallet and the planet.

While fresh fruits and veggies make delicious smoothies, don't shy away from frozen produce which can be just as nutritious, sometimes even more so. The produce is frozen at peak ripeness, locking in nutrients. Frozen banana chunks lend creaminess without needing ice. And you can find pre-chopped frozen greens that make throwing together a morning smoothie even easier.

That said, be mindful of added sugars in some frozen produce blends. Check the ingredients list and choose plain frozen fruits without added syrups. You can always sweeten with fresh bananas, dates, maple syrup, honey, or stevia to taste. If you struggle with PCOS, prediabetes, or diabetes, stick to lower glycemic fruits like berries and citrus fruits over tropical fruits when possible.

Smoothies can also help you get creative with using the pulp leftover from making nut milks and juices. Add almond pulp or oat pulp to smoothies for extra fiber, protein, and prebiotics. Pulp from juicing leafy greens, carrots, beets, or apples provides a budget-friendly way to include more produce. Just be sure to consume the pulp soon after juicing for maximum nutrition. Freezing veggie pulp in ice cube trays for future smoothies works too.

While smoothies make for quick and portable breakfasts, balance them with other whole foods like eggs, nuts, oatmeal, and yogurt for sustained energy. Smoothies that are predominantly fruit or juice without protein and fat can spike blood sugar. So include sources of protein and healthy fats, and avoid excessive fruit juice if you struggle with blood sugar regulation.

Portion control is also key when indulging in calorie-dense smoothies, especially for weight loss goals. As satisfying as they are, smoothies don't necessarily promote satiety due to their liquid form. Try diluting higher calorie smoothies with water, tea, or coconut water. Or halve the portion size and enjoy it as a pre-meal appetite tamer. Drinking smoothies mindfully through a straw instead of gulping can also curb overconsumption.

This is just the beginning of the vast world of morning smoothies. There are countless ingredient options and combinations to try based on your dietary needs, taste preferences, and health goals. Rotate your recipes to take advantage of the diverse array of nutrients in fruits, veggies, protein sources, healthy fats, and superfoods. Aim for balance and moderation. Most importantly, get creative with making smoothies your own. Soon you'll have a morning smoothie ritual that you look forward to each day.

Now that we've thoroughly explored morning smoothies, let's move on to discuss smoothies for the rest of the day and how to fuel your body optimally no matter the time. The upcoming chapter covers "Smoothies for Every Occasion: Recipes for Energy, Exercise, Weight Loss, and More." You'll find the ideal smoothie for pre and post-workout, midday snacks, meal replacements, healthy desserts, and much more. We'll also discuss targeting smoothies to meet specific wellness goals like glowing skin and improved digestion. Remember, smoothies aren't just for breakfast!

In the realm of healthy eating, few things rival the power and potential of green smoothies. At its core, a green smoothie is a drink made primarily from green leafy vegetables and fruits, blended together to create a nutrient-dense beverage that offers numerous health benefits.

Green Smoothie Revolution

The appeal of green smoothies lies in their nutritional profile. Green leafy vegetables are among the healthiest foods on the planet. They're packed with vitamins, minerals, antioxidants, and fiber, all of which are essential for overall health. When combined with fruits, which bring their own set of nutrients and a delightful sweetness, you get a beverage that's both delicious and beneficial to your health.

This chapter introduces the world of green smoothies, starting with the basics, understanding their benefits, and learning how to make them. The fundamentals of a good green smoothie lie in the balance between vegetables and fruits. Too many fruits can result in a sugar-laden drink, while too many vegetables may produce a taste that's less appealing.

The recipes in this chapter are designed to strike a balance between health and taste, making green smoothies a delightful part of your everyday diet. We'll start with simple, beginner-friendly recipes and gradually introduce more adventurous ingredients and combinations as we progress.

You'll learn to make classics like the 'Spinach Apple Delight', packed with iron from spinach and sweetness from apples, to more complex recipes like 'Kale Pineapple Ginger Bliss', a zesty, immunity-boosting concoction that combines the health benefits of kale with the tropical flavors of pineapple.

We'll also discuss the benefits of each ingredient, helping you understand the nutritional powerhouses that go into your smoothie. This knowledge will empower you to create your own smoothie recipes in the future, mixing and matching ingredients based on your nutritional needs and taste preferences.

Whether you're looking to kick-start your day with a burst of nutrients, seeking a mid-afternoon energy boost, or needing a post-workout recovery drink, green smoothies have you covered. Ready to start blending?

Mendocino Brock

Chapter 2

Supercharge Your Morning: Energizing Breakfast Smoothies

Smoothies have become an increasingly popular breakfast choice over the last few decades, offering a quick, portable, and nutritious start to the day. In Chapter 2 of the book "Supercharge Your Morning", we will explore the world of breakfast smoothies and how they can energize your mornings and set you up for success throughout the day.

The chapter begins by discussing the many benefits of drinking smoothies, especially as part of a balanced breakfast. Smoothies provide a concentrated dose of fruits, vegetables, protein, fiber and other nutrients that give you sustained energy, keep you feeling full and satisfied, and provide lasting focus and mental clarity. Unlike juice, smoothies retain all the fiber from the ingredients, which is important for digestive health, controlling blood sugar levels, and prolonging feelings of fullness. The portability of smoothies makes them ideal for busy mornings when you need nourishing food on the go.

After covering the advantages of smoothies, the chapter dives into the key components that make up a balanced, nutritious smoothie. It provides an overview of recommended fruits, vegetables, greens, proteins, healthy fats, and superfood add-ins to include. Fruits form the base of most smoothies and provide nutrients like vitamin C, antioxidants, and natural sugars for energy. Vegetables and greens amp up the nutritional value with vitamins, minerals, and phytonutrients while adding fiber. Proteins give smoothies staying power while healthy fats make them richer, creamier, and more satisfying. Superfoods like chia seeds, flaxseed, and maca powder boost the nutrient content even further.

Next, the chapter gives helpful tips for building the perfect smoothie. It covers guidance on choosing ripe fruits at their peak, preparing fresh greens properly, using frozen fruits and veggies for convenience and consistency, blending the ingredients in the right order, and achieving the ideal texture. Proper smoothie preparation brings out the full flavor and nutritional value of the ingredients. The chapter also advises on storing and transporting smoothies to maintain freshness and prevent separation or spoilage.

The bulk of the chapter features 25 mouthwatering energizing smoothie recipes specially crafted to power up your mornings. Each recipe lists the ingredients along with nutritional information so you can evaluate the protein content, calories, carbs, and more. The recipes encompass a wide range of flavors from sweet fruit blends to green veggie creations. Examples include:

Sunrise Strawberry Banana Smoothie

Mixed Berry Protein Powerhouse

Green Machine Spinach Smoothie

Peaches and Cream Oatmeal Smoothie

Cocoa Hazelnut Breakfast Smoothie

Carrot Cake Overnight Oats Smoothie

Blueberry Avocado Immunity Booster

The recipes specify preparation instructions including any advance steps needed for soaking nuts or making overnight oats. Handy variations are also provided to customize the smoothies to your own tastes and dietary needs, like swapping almond milk for cow's milk or adding extra protein powder.

To wrap up the chapter, the author summarizes the key benefits of breakfast smoothies and provides a concise step-by-step guide to building your own energizing smoothie. Some final tips are given for troubleshooting common smoothie issues like chalky texture or lack of creaminess. The author encourages readers to get creative with combinations and make smoothies part of their morning ritual for feeling focused, nourished, and ready to take on the day.

With its comprehensive advice, visual recipes, and vibrant photos, Chapter 2 will inspire you to supercharge your mornings with nutrient-dense, flavorful smoothies. Let's get blending!

The Importance of a Nutritious Breakfast

Breakfast is often hailed as the most important meal of the day. A well-balanced, nutrient-rich breakfast can set the tone for your day, giving you the energy you need to tackle your tasks and keeping you satiated to prevent overeating later. An energizing breakfast smoothie can be a quick and easy way to get the nutrition your body craves.

Why Breakfast Smoothies?

Breakfast smoothies are a perfect way to pack a multitude of nutrients into a single meal. They're easy to make, portable for those busy mornings, and can be prepared in advance for convenience. Plus, with the right combination of ingredients, they can provide a balance of carbohydrates, protein, and healthy fats to keep you fueled and satisfied.

Creating a Balanced Breakfast Smoothie

Building a balanced breakfast smoothie involves selecting ingredients that provide a mix of macronutrients. Carbohydrates from fruits and vegetables provide quick energy, protein helps to keep you satiated, and healthy fats promote nutrient absorption. A well-balanced smoothie can help prevent mid-morning energy crashes and cravings.

Recipe: Banana Oat Energizer

This smoothie combines the natural sweetness of banana with the heartiness of oats to create a drink that's both energizing and satisfying.

Greek yogurt adds a protein punch, while a spoonful of almond butter provides healthy fats.

Recipe: Green Tea Power Booster

Green tea adds a bit of caffeine to this power-packed smoothie, along with a host of antioxidants. Paired with spinach, avocado, and pineapple, this smoothie is a perfect morning pick-me-up.

Recipe: Berry Protein Blast

Berries bring a burst of flavor and antioxidants to this protein-packed smoothie. Greek yogurt and a scoop of your favorite protein powder ensure you're getting plenty of protein to start your day right.

Recipe: Tropical Morning Delight

This smoothie will make you feel like you're having breakfast in a tropical paradise. The combination of mango, pineapple, and coconut milk is not only delicious but also full of vitamins and healthy fats.

Maximizing Nutrient Absorption

Some nutrients are better absorbed when paired with others. For example, the fat-soluble vitamins A, D, E, and K are best absorbed when consumed with a source of fat. Adding a spoonful of nut butter or a splash of coconut milk to your smoothie can enhance the absorption of these vitamins.

Smoothie Prep Tips and Tricks

Preparing your smoothie ingredients in advance can make your morning routine even smoother. Learn tips for prepping and storing your ingredients, like freezing ripe fruit and portioning out your protein powder.

Keeping Your Morning Smoothies Varied and Exciting

To keep your breakfast smoothie routine from becoming monotonous, it's important to mix things up. Try experimenting with different fruits, types of greens, sources of protein, and healthy fats. You can also play around with adding various spices, like cinnamon or turmeric, for an extra boost of flavor and health benefits.

Recipe: Chocolate Morning Wake-up Call

For those with a sweet tooth, this smoothie is a dream come true. The smoothie features a ripe banana, a scoop of chocolate protein powder, a tablespoon of almond butter, and a cup of unsweetened almond milk. The banana and almond butter provide your body with both quick and sustained energy, while the protein powder keeps you satiated throughout the morning. Plus, who can resist the decadence of chocolate for breakfast?

Recipe: Veggie Powerhouse

If you're looking to incorporate more veggies into your breakfast, this smoothie is for you. Combining leafy greens like spinach or kale with a sweet apple, half an avocado, a scoop of vanilla protein powder, and a cup of almond milk creates a nutrient-packed breakfast that's both tasty and satisfying.

Understanding the Glycemic Impact of Your Smoothies

The glycemic index (GI) measures how quickly a food raises blood sugar levels. Foods with a high GI are digested quickly, causing a rapid rise in blood sugar, while low-GI foods are digested more slowly, leading to a more gradual rise in blood sugar. Many fruits have a low to moderate GI, making them a good choice for preventing blood sugar spikes. Pairing these fruits with a source of protein and fat can lower the overall GI of your smoothie.

Recipe: Low-Glycemic Green Monster

This smoothie features low-GI fruits like green apples and pears, combined with spinach, a scoop of protein powder, a tablespoon of chia seeds, and unsweetened almond milk. The result is a blood sugar-friendly smoothie that's as healthy as it is delicious.

Superfoods to Boost Your Breakfast Smoothie

Superfoods are nutritionally dense foods that offer various health benefits. Incorporating superfoods into your breakfast smoothie is an easy way to increase its nutrient content. Some superfoods you might consider adding include chia seeds for fiber and omega-3 fatty acids, turmeric for its anti-inflammatory properties, or goji berries for a dose of antioxidants.

Smoothie Add-Ins for Extra Nutrition

Along with superfoods, there are other ingredients you can add to your breakfast smoothie for extra nutrition. A spoonful of Greek yogurt adds a protein punch, a handful of oats provides lasting energy, and a splash of kefir gives a probiotic boost.

Adapting Your Smoothie to Dietary Restrictions

Whether you're vegan, gluten-free, dairy-free, or have other dietary restrictions, there are plenty of ways to adapt your breakfast smoothie. Plant-based protein powders, non-dairy milk alternatives, and gluten-free grains like quinoa or oats can all be used to create a smoothie that suits your needs.

Recipe: Apple Cinnamon Smoothie

Combining the comfort of apple pie and the health benefits of a smoothie, this recipe is a winner for colder mornings. All you need is a ripe apple, a banana, a scoop of vanilla protein powder, a teaspoon of cinnamon, a small handful of oats, and a cup of unsweetened almond milk. The result is a delightfully refreshing and hearty smoothie that keeps your taste buds satisfied and your stomach full.

Recipe: Immune-Boosting Citrus Delight

With the tartness of fresh citrus fruits and a zing of ginger, this smoothie not only helps you wake up but also boosts your immune system. You'll need the juice of two oranges, half a grapefruit, a small piece of fresh ginger, a tablespoon of honey, and ice cubes. This smoothie is vitamin C-rich and is excellent for those winter months when colds and flu are prevalent.

Building Smoothie Habits: Make It a Morning Ritual

Developing a habit of making a nutritious breakfast smoothie every morning can revolutionize your health and energy levels. Start with simple recipes and gradually try more complex ones as you get more comfortable. Remember, it's all about taking small steps towards a healthier lifestyle.

Protein Powders: How to Choose the Right One

Protein powders can be a convenient way to increase the protein content of your smoothies. However, the multitude of options can be overwhelming. In this section, we'll discuss the various types of protein powders available—whey, plant-based, casein—and how to choose the best one for your needs.

Understanding Smoothie Textures

The texture of your smoothie can make a big difference in your enjoyment. Whether you prefer a thicker, spoonable smoothie bowl or a thinner, drinkable smoothie, understanding how different ingredients affect the texture can help you create your perfect smoothie.

The Art of Layering Flavors

Making a great-tasting smoothie isn't just about throwing a bunch of ingredients into a blender. It's also about understanding how different flavors work together. Learn how to balance sweet, tart, and neutral flavors to create a smoothie that tickles your taste buds.

Fruits and Their Nutritional Profiles

Different fruits bring different flavors and nutritional benefits to your smoothies. Learn more about the nutrients that various fruits provide—from the potassium in bananas to the vitamin C in oranges—and how to best combine them in your smoothies.
Taking Your Smoothie on the Go

Busy mornings shouldn't keep you from enjoying a nutrient-dense breakfast. For those mornings when you're on the go, a travel-friendly smoothie cup can be a lifesaver. You can blend your smoothie right before you leave and take it with you, ensuring that even the busiest of days start with a good meal.

Smoothie Meal Prep

Setting aside a little time during your weekend to prepare smoothie ingredients can make your weekday mornings run a lot smoother. From chopping and freezing fruits and vegetables to pre-portioning dry ingredients in small containers or zip-top bags, meal prepping can be a game-changer.

The Role of Greens in Your Morning Smoothie

Adding a handful of greens to your morning smoothie can be an easy way to increase your daily vegetable intake. Spinach, kale, and chard are all great options. They not only bring a host of health benefits but also, when paired with the right fruits, they don't overpower the smoothie's taste.

Recipe: Avocado Green Dream

Avocado adds a creamy richness to smoothies that's hard to beat. For this recipe, blend half an avocado with a handful of spinach, a ripe banana, a spoonful of honey, and a cup of unsweetened almond milk. The result is a silky, satisfying smoothie that's packed with healthy fats and leafy green goodness.

Recipe: Sunrise Beet and Berry

Beets bring a lovely color and a load of nutrients to your morning smoothie. For this recipe, you'll need half a small beet, a cup of mixed berries, a small ripe banana, a cup of Greek yogurt, and a dash of honey. This smoothie is as beautiful as it is delicious and healthy.

Using Nuts and Seeds in Your Smoothies

Nuts and seeds can provide a boost of protein and healthy fats to your morning smoothies. Learn about the health benefits of popular options such as almonds, flax seeds, chia seeds, and cashews, and discover how to best incorporate them into your smoothies.

Green Smoothie Revolution

Smoothies vs. Juices: The Benefits of Keeping the Fiber

While fruit juices can be part of a healthy diet, smoothies have an advantage: they retain the fiber from the fruits and vegetables, which helps keep you feeling fuller longer. This section will delve deeper into the benefits of keeping the fiber in your morning drink.

By the end of this chapter, you'll not only have a repertoire of delicious breakfast smoothie recipes but also a comprehensive understanding of the nutritional aspects of your morning meal. The next time your alarm goes off, you can look forward to kick-starting your day with a homemade smoothie that's as delicious as it is nourishing.

As we close out this chapter on energizing breakfast smoothies, let's recap the key benefits of adding these nutritious blended beverages into your morning routine:

Smoothies provide an easy way to pack a concentrated punch of fruits, vegetables, protein, fiber and healthy fats into one portable meal. All those nutrients give you sustained energy to tackle the day ahead. The natural sugars in fruits get metabolized slowly and steadily with the fiber, keeping your blood sugar balanced. That means no mid-morning crash! The combo of protein, fat, and fiber also keeps you feeling satiated and focused so you aren't distracted by hunger.

Drinking a smoothie makes getting your daily dose of fruits and veggies effortless. You can cram in servings from across the color spectrum, loading up on a rainbow of phytonutrients, antioxidants, and vitamins. Smoothies are also a great way to get picky eaters or kids to consume more greens. Simply mask the flavor with sweet fruits and milks.

Meal prepping smoothies takes the stress out of morning routines. You can prep ingredients in advance, or batch blend a few servings of smoothies to grab and go all week long. Having a smoothie ready to chill in the fridge makes it that much easier to skip sugary cereals or pastries when you're rushed. They're portable for drinking on the commute to work or school. No more waiting in line for overpriced lattes!

Customizing your own smoothies allows you to cater to your personal nutritional needs and taste preferences. Add extra protein if you're looking to build muscle. Toss in chia or flax seeds for omega-3's. Or go dairy-free with non-dairy milks and yogurts. Prepare them to your desired thickness or creaminess. The options are endless.

While the recipes in this chapter are a great starting point, don't be afraid to get creative and substitute your own favorite fruits, veggies, and superfoods. The key is combining the fundamental smoothie elements - fruit for sweetness, leafy greens or veggies for nutrients, protein for satiety, healthy fats for richness, and a liquid base. Herbs, spices, nut butters, and seeds can take your smoothies to the next level.

Hopefully this chapter has shown how easy and enjoyable it can be to make smoothies that energize your mornings. They beat out sugary cereal or carb-heavy muffins any day when it comes to a balanced breakfast that provides sustained energy. Just a few minutes of prep the night before means you're ready to blend and savor a nutritious, delicious smoothie in the morning.

Keep experimenting with new flavor combos and ingredient additions to find your perfect energizing smoothies. Try out the recipes in this chapter, but also feel free to substitute and customize to your taste. Share your favorite smoothie creations on social media and inspire others to energize their mornings too.

Remember, smoothies are highly adaptable to your personal diet. Modify them to be vegetarian, vegan, dairy-free, nut-free or high-protein. Rotate seasonal fruits and veggies. Let your imagination run wild!

Blend up a smoothie in the morning and note the difference in how you feel throughout the day - focused, satisfied, and energized until lunchtime. Here's to many mornings ahead supercharged by nourishing, vibrant smoothies!

Chapter 3
The Perfect Post-Workout: Recovery Smoothies

After a hard workout, your body needs the right nutrients to recover and rebuild muscle. A post-workout smoothie is the perfect way to refuel your body with protein, carbs, vitamins, and minerals. In this chapter, we'll explore 10 nutritious and delicious smoothie recipes specifically designed for post-workout recovery.

First, let's look at why recovery smoothies are so important. During exercise, your muscles use up their glycogen stores for energy. Glycogen is the main storage form of carbs in the muscles and liver. Intense exercise can almost empty out these glycogen stores. Replenishing them is crucial for muscle repair and growth. Protein is also broken down during exercise, so consuming protein after a workout provides the amino acids needed to rebuild and strengthen muscle fibers.

Smoothies make an ideal post-workout snack because they are easy to digest. After an intense workout, the last thing you want is to feel heavy and bloated. The liquid format of smoothies allows for fast absorption of nutrients. Smoothies also provide hydration to replace fluids lost through sweat.

Now let's explore the key ingredients for recovery smoothies. Whey protein powder contains essential amino acids for muscle protein synthesis. Look for a high-quality whey isolate for maximum protein with little to no carbs or fat. Bananas provide potassium, an electrolyte lost through sweat. The simple carbs in bananas also help replenish glycogen stores. Greek yogurt adds protein plus probiotics to support immunity and digestion. Frozen berries like blueberries and raspberries offer antioxidant power to reduce inflammation. Leafy greens like spinach provide vitamins and minerals like vitamin C, calcium, and iron.

The smoothie recipes in this chapter combine the perfect blends of these nutrient-dense ingredients. Let's look at 10 delicious options:

Chocolate Peanut Butter - Banana, cocoa powder, peanut butter, protein powder, milk

Strawberry Shortcake - Greek yogurt, strawberries, vanilla protein powder, oats

Green Machine - Spinach, mango, banana, vanilla Greek yogurt, juice

Blueberry Cobbler - Blueberries, cherry Greek yogurt, cinnamon, oats

Banana Bread - Banana, almond butter, cinnamon, almond milk, protein powder 6.Cookies and Cream - Banana, cacao nibs, peanut butter, chocolate protein powder, milk

Pineapple Coconut - Pineapple, coconut water, vanilla Greek yogurt, coconut flakes

Chocolate Cherry - Cherries, cacao powder, chocolate protein powder, almond milk

Berry Almond - Mixed berries, almond butter, vanilla protein powder, almond milk

Mint Chocolate Chip - Spinach, banana, mint, cacao nibs, chocolate protein powder, milk

With this wide variety of flavors and ingredient combinations, you'll look forward to your post-workout smoothie. The important thing is to consume a smoothie within 45 minutes after exercise when nutrient uptake is maximized. Keep trial sizes of protein powder and frozen fruits at the gym for a quick shake.

Understanding Post-Workout Nutrition

After you exercise, your body is primed to receive and utilize nutrients to start the recovery process. Consuming a combination of carbohydrates and protein within a specific window can facilitate quicker recovery and promote muscle growth. This section will delve deeper into the science behind post-workout nutrition and how it affects recovery.

Recipe: Berry Blast Recovery Smoothie

This smoothie is a blend of frozen mixed berries, a banana for added sweetness and carbs, plain Greek yogurt for protein, and a splash of almond milk. The result is a refreshing, protein-rich smoothie that also delivers a healthy dose of antioxidants from the berries.

Using Protein Powders for Recovery

Protein powders can be an excellent addition to recovery smoothies. They deliver a concentrated dose of protein that helps repair and build muscles after a workout. Whether you prefer whey protein, a plant-based option, or casein, there's a protein powder to fit your needs and dietary preferences.

Recipe: Tropical Protein Punch

This tropical-inspired recovery smoothie features a scoop of your preferred protein powder, a cup of frozen mango chunks, half a banana, a handful of spinach, and coconut water. This recipe is a delightful way to deliver protein to your muscles while also providing replenishing electrolytes from the coconut water.

Benefits of Including Healthy Fats in Recovery Smoothies

While protein and carbohydrates often take center stage in post-workout nutrition, healthy fats also play a role in recovery. Healthy fats help reduce inflammation and are necessary for the absorption of fat-soluble vitamins. Adding a source of healthy fats—like avocados, nuts, or seeds—can boost the nutritional value of your recovery smoothie.

Recipe: Chocolate Avocado Recovery Smoothie

Green Smoothie Revolution

This smoothie blends half an avocado with a banana, a scoop of chocolate protein powder, a tablespoon of unsweetened cocoa powder, a teaspoon of honey, and almond milk. The result is a creamy, decadent recovery smoothie that's packed with protein, healthy fats, and a rich chocolate flavor.

Adding Electrolytes to Your Smoothie

After a sweaty workout session, replacing lost electrolytes is important. While sports drinks can serve this purpose, they often contain added sugars and artificial flavors. Learn how to use natural ingredients—like coconut water, bananas, and oranges—to add electrolytes to your recovery smoothies.

Recipe: Hydrating Citrus and Coconut Smoothie

This electrolyte-packed smoothie uses coconut water as a base and blends it with an orange, half a grapefruit, a handful of spinach, and a scoop of vanilla protein powder. The result is a hydrating, nutrient-dense recovery smoothie with a fresh citrus taste.

Smoothies for Different Types of Workouts

Different types of workouts—like weightlifting, endurance training, or high-intensity interval training (HIIT)—may require different post-workout nutrition strategies. This section will provide guidance on how to adjust your recovery smoothie to best suit your exercise routine.

Dairy vs. Non-Dairy Smoothies for Recovery

Dairy products like milk and Greek yogurt are excellent sources of protein and can be great for recovery smoothies. However, if you are lactose intolerant, vegan, or prefer to avoid dairy for any other reason, there are many non-dairy alternatives. Learn about the pros and cons of both and how to make delicious recovery smoothies with each type.

Recipe: Creamy Cashew and Banana Smoothie

For a dairy-free recovery smoothie, blend together a ripe banana, a handful of cashews, a scoop of plant-based protein powder, a teaspoon of honey, and a cup of unsweetened almond milk. The result is a smooth, protein-packed smoothie with a mild, pleasing taste.

Importance of Hydration in Recovery

Even mild dehydration can impair recovery and performance. Therefore, ensuring that your recovery smoothie aids in hydration is key. This section will discuss the role of hydration in recovery and how to maximize the hydration potential of your smoothies.

Recipe: Cucumber Melon Hydration Smoothie

For a hydrating recovery smoothie, blend together a cup of cubed melon (like cantaloupe or honeydew), half a cucumber, a scoop of vanilla protein powder, a dash of honey, and coconut water. This smoothie is refreshingly light and packed with hydrating ingredients.

Adding Superfoods for Extra Nutrient Boost

Superfoods like chia seeds, flax seeds, spirulina, and goji berries can provide additional nutrients to your recovery smoothies. Learn more about the health benefits of these superfoods and how to incorporate them into your smoothies.

Recipe: Berry and Chia Seed Power Smoothie

For this superfood-infused recovery smoothie, blend together a cup of mixed berries, a banana, a tablespoon of chia seeds, a scoop of protein powder, and almond milk. The chia seeds not only add a nutrient boost but also help thicken the smoothie, creating a satisfying texture.

The Role of Antioxidants in Recovery

Intense exercise can produce free radicals, which can lead to oxidative stress if not balanced by antioxidants. Consuming antioxidants after a workout can help mitigate this. Fruits and vegetables are excellent sources of antioxidants, making them great additions to recovery smoothies.

Recipe: Antioxidant-Rich Berry and Spinach Smoothie

This recovery smoothie packs an antioxidant punch with a cup of mixed berries, a handful of spinach, a banana, a scoop of protein powder, and almond milk. It's a fruity, nutritious way to boost your antioxidant intake post-workout.

The Role of Carbs in Recovery

While protein is often the focus in post-workout nutrition, carbohydrates also play an essential role. They help replenish the glycogen stores in your muscles, which is your body's main source of energy during exercise. In this section, you'll learn more about the types of carbohydrates best suited for post-workout recovery and how to incorporate them into your smoothies.

Recipe: Sweet Potato Pie Recovery Smoothie

For a high-carb recovery smoothie, blend together half a cooked sweet potato, a banana, a scoop of vanilla protein powder, a teaspoon of cinnamon, and unsweetened almond milk. This smoothie not only helps restore your glycogen levels but also tastes like a dessert in a glass.

Adding Flavor Without Adding Sugar

While some natural sugars from fruits are beneficial in recovery smoothies, it's essential to avoid adding too much extra sugar. This section will teach you how to use ingredients like spices, cacao powder, and unsweetened nut butters to add flavor to your smoothies without relying on added sugars.

Recipe: Spiced Pear and Almond Butter Smoothie

For this flavorful, no-added-sugar recovery smoothie, blend together a ripe pear, a scoop of protein powder, a tablespoon of almond butter, a sprinkle of nutmeg and cinnamon, and unsweetened almond milk. The result is a nutrient-dense smoothie with the comforting taste of spiced pear.

Proper Timing for Post-Workout Smoothies

While it's beneficial to consume your recovery smoothie soon after a workout, the ideal timing can depend on various factors, including the intensity of your workout, your overall diet, and your individual needs. This section will guide you on how to determine the best timing for your post-workout smoothies.

Balancing Your Diet With Recovery Smoothies

While recovery smoothies can be a great addition to your diet, they shouldn't replace balanced, whole-food meals. Learn how to use recovery smoothies as part of a balanced diet and how to avoid common pitfalls, such as relying too heavily on smoothies for your nutritional needs.

Recipe: Balanced Green Recovery Smoothie

For a balanced recovery smoothie, blend together a handful of spinach, a small avocado, a ripe banana, a scoop of protein powder, a tablespoon of flax seeds, and unsweetened almond milk. This smoothie provides a good balance of protein, carbs, healthy fats, and greens.

Understanding Liquid Bases for Recovery Smoothies

The liquid base you choose for your smoothie can significantly impact its nutritional content, taste, and consistency. This section will provide a detailed comparison of popular choices like milk, almond milk, coconut water, and yogurt, along with tips on selecting the best base for your recovery smoothie.

Recipe: Soothing Oat Milk and Cherry Smoothie

For a creamy recovery smoothie with a unique flavor profile, blend together a cup of pitted cherries, a ripe banana, a scoop of vanilla protein powder, a tablespoon of chia seeds, and oat milk. Cherries are known for their anti-inflammatory properties, making this smoothie a great choice for muscle recovery.

Addressing Dietary Restrictions and Allergies

Whether you're lactose intolerant, gluten intolerant, vegan, or have other dietary restrictions or allergies, you can still make delicious and nutritious recovery smoothies. This section will provide strategies and ingredient swaps to ensure everyone can enjoy the benefits of recovery smoothies.

Green Smoothie Revolution

Recipe: Gluten-Free Blueberry Muffin Smoothie

For a gluten-free recovery smoothie, blend together a cup of frozen blueberries, half a cooked and cooled sweet potato, a scoop of plant-based protein powder, a tablespoon of ground flaxseed, a teaspoon of cinnamon, and unsweetened almond milk. It's like enjoying a blueberry muffin in a glass, minus the gluten.

Customizing Your Recovery Smoothie

One of the great things about smoothies is their versatility. Once you understand the basic formula for a recovery smoothie, you can start to experiment with different ingredients to suit your taste and nutritional needs. This section will provide guidance on creating your own recovery smoothie recipes.

Recipe: Customizable Green Recovery Smoothie

For a highly customizable recovery smoothie, start with a handful of your favorite leafy greens, add a source of protein (like Greek yogurt or protein powder), choose a carb source (like a banana or an apple), add a healthy fat (like avocado or flaxseeds), and choose your liquid base. The options are endless, and the result is a recovery smoothie tailored just for you.

The Art of Smoothie Prep

Making a recovery smoothie after a tiring workout can seem like a daunting task. That's where smoothie prep comes in. This section will guide you through the process of prepping your smoothie ingredients in advance, so all you have to do after your workout is blend and enjoy.

By the end of this chapter, you'll have an extensive knowledge of post-workout recovery nutrition and a wide variety of recovery smoothie recipes at your fingertips. With this information, you'll be able to optimize your post-workout recovery, fuel your muscles effectively, and enjoy a tasty treat after your workout sessions. Whether you're an athlete or a fitness enthusiast, recovery smoothies can play a key role in your fitness journey, and this chapter will serve as your comprehensive guide.

Mendocino Brock

Chapter 4

Dinner in a Glass: Savory Smoothies for the Evening

Savory smoothies may sound unusual if you're used to the sweet fruit-based smoothies. However, they can be a refreshing change and a great way to incorporate more vegetables into your diet. In this section, you'll learn about the key components of a savory smoothie and why you might want to give them a try.

Recipe: Refreshing Cucumber and Avocado Smoothie

To kickstart your savory smoothie journey, try blending together a cucumber, half an avocado, a handful of spinach, a pinch of sea salt, a squeeze of lemon juice, and some cold water. The result is a refreshing, creamy, and surprisingly satisfying smoothie, perfect for a light evening meal.

The Role of Herbs and Spices in Savory Smoothies

Herbs and spices can turn a bland smoothie into a flavorful delight. From basil and cilantro to turmeric and cayenne pepper, you'll learn about the different herbs and spices you can use in your savory smoothies and their health benefits.

Recipe: Spicy Tomato and Bell Pepper Smoothie

For a savory smoothie with a kick, blend together a ripe tomato, half a red bell pepper, a handful of spinach, a small clove of garlic, a pinch of cayenne pepper, some fresh basil, and vegetable broth. This smoothie is like a gazpacho in a glass and is full of antioxidants and vitamins.

Nutritional Benefits of Savory Smoothies

Green Smoothie Revolution

While all smoothies can be healthy if made with the right ingredients, savory smoothies often pack in more vegetables and fewer sugars. This section will delve into the nutritional benefits of savory smoothies and why they can make a great dinner option.

Recipe: Nutrient-Packed Green Goddess Smoothie

For a super nutritious savory smoothie, blend together a handful of kale, half an avocado, a small cucumber, a stalk of celery, some fresh parsley, a squeeze of lemon juice, a spoonful of nutritional yeast, and cold water. This smoothie is a powerhouse of vitamins, minerals, and fiber, making it a wonderful, nutrient-dense dinner choice.

Satisfying Your Hunger With Savory Smoothies

Savory smoothies can be just as filling as any other meal if you know how to build them right. This section will teach you about adding protein, healthy fats, and fiber to your savory smoothies to keep you satisfied throughout the evening.

Recipe: Hearty Lentil and Vegetable Smoothie

To make a filling savory smoothie, blend together half a cup of cooked lentils, a carrot, a handful of spinach, a small tomato, a clove of garlic, some fresh basil, and vegetable broth. The lentils provide a good dose of protein and fiber, making this smoothie a substantial meal.

Pairing Savory Smoothies with Other Foods

While a savory smoothie can be a complete meal on its own, sometimes you might want to pair it with something else for a more rounded dinner. This section will give you ideas on what foods pair well with savory smoothies.

Recipe: Creamy Avocado and Spinach Smoothie with Toasted Nuts

For a savory smoothie that pairs well with other foods, try blending together half an avocado, a handful of spinach, a small cucumber, some fresh dill, a squeeze of lemon juice, and almond milk. Top it with some toasted nuts for added crunch and serve it alongside a piece of grilled chicken or a slice of whole grain bread.

Creating a Balanced Savory Smoothie

Creating a balanced savory smoothie isn't just about tossing vegetables into a blender. It involves carefully choosing ingredients that work well together in terms of flavor and nutrition. In this section, we'll dive deeper into how to balance your savory smoothie ingredients to achieve a harmonious blend of tastes and a nutrient-dense result.

Recipe: Roasted Beetroot and Carrot Smoothie

For a well-balanced savory smoothie, try blending together a small roasted beetroot, a roasted carrot, half an avocado, a handful of spinach, a spoonful of tahini, a splash of apple cider vinegar, and vegetable broth. The roasted vegetables provide a deep, sweet flavor that balances perfectly with the tangy vinegar and creamy tahini and avocado.

Experimenting with Texture in Savory Smoothies

The texture of a smoothie can make or break your enjoyment of it. From creamy to chunky, and everything in between, this section will guide you on how to experiment with texture in your savory smoothies.

Recipe: Chunky Gazpacho-Style Smoothie

For a chunky, gazpacho-style smoothie, blend together a ripe tomato, a cucumber, a small bell pepper, a small onion, a clove of garlic, a splash of red wine vinegar, and a drizzle of olive oil, but only until coarsely pureed. Add some finely diced cucumber and bell pepper for extra crunch, and serve chilled.

Adding Superfoods to Your Savory Smoothies

Superfoods can provide your savory smoothies with an extra boost of nutrition. This section will cover a variety of superfoods, like chia seeds, flax seeds, spirulina, and turmeric, and how to incorporate them into your savory smoothies.

Recipe: Turmeric and Ginger Veggie Smoothie

For a superfood-packed savory smoothie, blend together a handful of kale, a small cucumber, a piece of fresh turmeric, a piece of fresh ginger, a spoonful of chia seeds, a squeeze of lemon juice, and coconut water. This smoothie is not only packed with antioxidants and anti-inflammatory compounds but also has a vibrant, refreshing flavor.

Mastering the Art of Smoothie Bowls

Smoothie bowls can offer a fun and satisfying twist to your standard smoothie. With a thicker texture and a variety of toppings, they can turn your savory smoothie into a spoonable meal. This section will guide you on how to make the perfect smoothie bowl.

Recipe: Green Goddess Smoothie Bowl

To make a smoothie bowl, blend together a handful of spinach, half an avocado, a small cucumber, a spoonful of hemp seeds, some fresh basil, a squeeze of lemon juice, and a small amount of almond milk, until thick and creamy. Pour it into a bowl and top with sliced avocado, cherry tomatoes, and a sprinkle of sesame seeds.

Experimenting with Savory Smoothie Toppings

Just like with smoothie bowls, adding toppings to your savory smoothies can add extra flavor, texture, and nutrition. In this section, you will learn about different types of toppings you can use, including seeds, nuts, herbs, spices, and even certain types of cheese.

Recipe: Tomato and Basil Smoothie with Feta Cheese

Blend together a ripe tomato, half a bell pepper, a small cucumber, a handful of fresh basil leaves, a splash of red wine vinegar, a drizzle of olive oil, and a cup of cold water. Once smooth, pour into a glass and top with crumbled feta cheese and a few extra basil leaves. The feta adds a salty, tangy flavor that complements the fresh and zesty smoothie perfectly.

Making Your Savory Smoothies More Filling

While savory smoothies are already quite satisfying due to their high fiber content, there are ways to make them even more filling. This section will discuss adding ingredients like cooked grains, legumes, and starchy vegetables to your smoothies.

Recipe: Butternut Squash and Lentil Smoothie

For a truly hearty savory smoothie, blend together a cup of roasted butternut squash, half a cup of cooked red lentils, a small carrot, a handful of spinach, a piece of fresh ginger, a spoonful of tahini, and vegetable broth. The result is a thick, creamy smoothie that's as satisfying as a bowl of soup.

Savory Smoothies for Specific Dietary Needs

Whether you're vegetarian, vegan, or following a specific diet like Paleo or Keto, savory smoothies can be easily adapted to fit your dietary needs. This section will provide tips and ingredient swaps for various diets.

Recipe: Keto-Friendly Avocado and Spinach Smoothie

For a keto-friendly savory smoothie, blend together a whole avocado, a handful of spinach, a small cucumber, a spoonful of chia seeds, a squeeze of lime juice, and a cup of unsweetened almond milk. High in healthy fats and low in carbs, this smoothie fits perfectly into a keto diet.

The Science of Food Pairing in Savory Smoothies

The food pairing technique involves combining foods that share key flavor compounds, resulting in a harmonious taste experience. This section will explore the science of food pairing in the context of savory smoothies, helping you create more flavorful combinations.

Recipe: Sweet Potato and Cinnamon Smoothie

For an example of food pairing in action, blend together a small cooked sweet potato, a small carrot, a piece of fresh ginger, a dash of cinnamon, a spoonful of almond butter, and almond milk. The sweet potato and cinnamon share key flavor compounds, making this smoothie surprisingly delicious.

Benefits of Meal Prepping Your Savory Smoothies

In a fast-paced world, meal prepping is an effective strategy to save time, reduce stress, and ensure you maintain healthy eating habits. The good news is, savory smoothies lend themselves perfectly to meal prep. This section will provide you with the basics of meal prepping your savory smoothies.

Recipe: Kale and Bean Smoothie Prep Packs

Create your own smoothie prep packs by portioning out all your ingredients beforehand. For a kale and bean smoothie, portion out a handful of kale, half a can of white beans, a small cucumber, a spoonful of hemp seeds, and a pinch of salt in separate containers or ziplock bags. When you're ready to make your smoothie, just empty your pack into the blender, add water or broth, and blend until smooth.

Exploring International Flavors in Savory Smoothies

Savory smoothies offer a great platform to explore and experiment with flavors from around the world. This section will guide you through various international flavor profiles and how to incorporate them into your smoothies.

Recipe: Thai-Style Savory Smoothie

For a Thai-inspired savory smoothie, blend together a small cucumber, a small piece of fresh ginger, a handful of cilantro, a squeeze of lime juice, a spoonful of peanut butter, a pinch of chili flakes, and coconut water. The result is a refreshing smoothie that echoes the flavors of a Thai salad.

Pairing Your Savory Smoothies with Other Dishes

While savory smoothies can certainly be enjoyed on their own, sometimes it can be nice to pair them with other dishes. This section will provide you with some ideas on what to pair your savory smoothies with.

Recipe: Bell Pepper and Tomato Smoothie with Grilled Cheese

Blend together a red bell pepper, a ripe tomato, a small onion, a clove of garlic, a splash of red wine vinegar, and a drizzle of olive oil. Pair this smoothie with a classic grilled cheese sandwich for a comforting and balanced meal.

How to Make Your Savory Smoothies Look As Good As They Taste

We eat with our eyes first, so making your smoothies look good is just as important as making them taste good. This section will give you tips on how to make your savory smoothies look appealing, from choosing colorful ingredients to serving them in stylish glasses or bowls.

Recipe: Rainbow Vegetable Smoothie

To create a visually striking smoothie, select vegetables of different colors, such as a small beetroot, a carrot, a yellow bell pepper, a cucumber, and a handful of spinach. Blend each vegetable individually with a little water or broth, then layer them in a tall glass to create a rainbow effect.Savory smoothies may sound unusual if you're used to the sweet fruit-based smoothies. However, they can be a refreshing change and a great way to incorporate more vegetables into your diet. In this section, you'll learn about the key components of a savory smoothie and why you might want to give them a try.

Recipe: Refreshing Cucumber and Avocado Smoothie

To kickstart your savory smoothie journey, try blending together a cucumber, half an avocado, a handful of spinach, a pinch of sea salt, a squeeze of lemon juice, and some cold water. The result is a refreshing, creamy, and surprisingly satisfying smoothie, perfect for a light evening meal.

The Role of Herbs and Spices in Savory Smoothies

Herbs and spices can turn a bland smoothie into a flavorful delight. From basil and cilantro to turmeric and cayenne pepper, you'll learn about the different herbs and spices you can use in your savory smoothies and their health benefits.

Green Smoothie Revolution

Recipe: Spicy Tomato and Bell Pepper Smoothie

For a savory smoothie with a kick, blend together a ripe tomato, half a red bell pepper, a handful of spinach, a small clove of garlic, a pinch of cayenne pepper, some fresh basil, and vegetable broth. This smoothie is like a gazpacho in a glass and is full of antioxidants and vitamins.

Nutritional Benefits of Savory Smoothies

While all smoothies can be healthy if made with the right ingredients, savory smoothies often pack in more vegetables and fewer sugars. This section will delve into the nutritional benefits of savory smoothies and why they can make a great dinner option.

Recipe: Nutrient-Packed Green Goddess Smoothie

For a super nutritious savory smoothie, blend together a handful of kale, half an avocado, a small cucumber, a stalk of celery, some fresh parsley, a squeeze of lemon juice, a spoonful of nutritional yeast, and cold water. This smoothie is a powerhouse of vitamins, minerals, and fiber, making it a wonderful, nutrient-dense dinner choice.

Satisfying Your Hunger With Savory Smoothies

Savory smoothies can be just as filling as any other meal if you know how to build them right. This section will teach you about adding protein, healthy fats, and fiber to your savory smoothies to keep you satisfied throughout the evening.

Recipe: Hearty Lentil and Vegetable Smoothie

To make a filling savory smoothie, blend together half a cup of cooked lentils, a carrot, a handful of spinach, a small tomato, a clove of garlic, some fresh basil, and vegetable broth. The lentils provide a good dose of protein and fiber, making this smoothie a substantial meal.

Pairing Savory Smoothies with Other Foods

While a savory smoothie can be a complete meal on its own, sometimes you might want to pair it with something else for a more rounded dinner. This section will give you ideas on what foods pair well with savory smoothies.

Recipe: Creamy Avocado and Spinach Smoothie with Toasted Nuts

For a savory smoothie that pairs well with other foods, try blending together half an avocado, a handful of spinach, a small cucumber, some fresh dill, a squeeze of lemon juice, and almond milk. Top it with some toasted nuts for added crunch and serve it alongside a piece of grilled chicken or a slice of whole grain bread.

Creating a Balanced Savory Smoothie

Creating a balanced savory smoothie isn't just about tossing vegetables into a blender. It involves carefully choosing ingredients that work well together in terms of flavor and nutrition. In this section, we'll dive deeper into how to balance your savory smoothie ingredients to achieve a harmonious blend of tastes and a nutrient-dense result.

Recipe: Roasted Beetroot and Carrot Smoothie

For a well-balanced savory smoothie, try blending together a small roasted beetroot, a roasted carrot, half an avocado, a handful of spinach, a spoonful of tahini, a splash of apple cider vinegar, and vegetable broth. The roasted vegetables provide a deep, sweet flavor that balances perfectly with the tangy vinegar and creamy tahini and avocado.

Experimenting with Texture in Savory Smoothies

The texture of a smoothie can make or break your enjoyment of it. From creamy to chunky, and everything in between, this section will guide you on how to experiment with texture in your savory smoothies.

Recipe: Chunky Gazpacho-Style Smoothie

For a chunky, gazpacho-style smoothie, blend together a ripe tomato, a cucumber, a small bell pepper, a small onion, a clove of garlic, a splash of red wine vinegar, and a drizzle of olive oil, but only until coarsely pureed. Add some finely diced cucumber and bell pepper for extra crunch, and serve chilled.

Adding Superfoods to Your Savory Smoothies

Superfoods can provide your savory smoothies with an extra boost of nutrition. This section will cover a variety of superfoods, like chia seeds, flax seeds, spirulina, and turmeric, and how to incorporate them into your savory smoothies.

Recipe: Turmeric and Ginger Veggie Smoothie

For a superfood-packed savory smoothie, blend together a handful of kale, a small cucumber, a piece of fresh turmeric, a piece of fresh ginger, a spoonful of chia seeds, a squeeze of lemon juice, and coconut water. This smoothie is not only packed with antioxidants and anti-inflammatory compounds but also has a vibrant, refreshing flavor.

Mastering the Art of Smoothie Bowls

Smoothie bowls can offer a fun and satisfying twist to your standard smoothie. With a thicker texture and a variety of toppings, they can turn your savory smoothie into a spoonable meal. This section will guide you on how to make the perfect smoothie bowl.

Recipe: Green Goddess Smoothie Bowl

To make a smoothie bowl, blend together a handful of spinach, half an avocado, a small cucumber, a spoonful of hemp seeds, some fresh basil, a squeeze of lemon juice, and a small amount of almond milk, until thick and creamy. Pour it into a bowl and top with sliced avocado, cherry tomatoes, and a sprinkle of sesame seeds.

Experimenting with Savory Smoothie Toppings

Just like with smoothie bowls, adding toppings to your savory smoothies can add extra flavor, texture, and nutrition. In this section, you will learn about different types of toppings you can use, including seeds, nuts, herbs, spices, and even certain types of cheese.

Mendocino Brock

Recipe: Tomato and Basil Smoothie with Feta Cheese

Blend together a ripe tomato, half a bell pepper, a handful of fresh basil leaves, a splash of red wine vinegar, a drizzle of olive oil, and a cup of cold water. Once smooth, pour into a glass and top with crumbled feta cheese and a few extra basil leaves. The feta adds a salty, tangy flavor that complements the fresh and zesty smoothie perfectly.

Making Your Savory Smoothies More Filling

While savory smoothies are already quite satisfying due to their high fiber content, there are ways to make them even more filling. This section will discuss adding ingredients like cooked grains, legumes, and starchy vegetables to your smoothies.

Recipe: Butternut Squash and Lentil Smoothie

For a truly hearty savory smoothie, blend together a cup of roasted butternut squash, half a cup of cooked red lentils, a small carrot, a handful of spinach, a piece of fresh ginger, a spoonful of tahini, and vegetable broth. The result is a thick, creamy smoothie that's as satisfying as a bowl of soup.

Savory Smoothies for Specific Dietary Needs

Whether you're vegetarian, vegan, or following a specific diet like Paleo or Keto, savory smoothies can be easily adapted to fit your dietary needs. This section will provide tips and ingredient swaps for various diets.

Recipe: Keto-Friendly Avocado and Spinach Smoothie

For a keto-friendly savory smoothie, blend together a whole avocado, a handful of spinach, a small cucumber, a spoonful of chia seeds, a squeeze of lime juice, and a cup of unsweetened almond milk. High in healthy fats and low in carbs, this smoothie fits perfectly into a keto diet.

The Science of Food Pairing in Savory Smoothies

Green Smoothie Revolution

The food pairing technique involves combining foods that share key flavor compounds, resulting in a harmonious taste experience. This section will explore the science of food pairing in the context of savory smoothies, helping you create more flavorful combinations.

Recipe: Sweet Potato and Cinnamon Smoothie

For an example of food pairing in action, blend together a small cooked sweet potato, a small carrot, a piece of fresh ginger, a dash of cinnamon, a spoonful of almond butter, and almond milk. The sweet potato and cinnamon share key flavor compounds, making this smoothie surprisingly delicious.

Benefits of Meal Prepping Your Savory Smoothies

In a fast-paced world, meal prepping is an effective strategy to save time, reduce stress, and ensure you maintain healthy eating habits. The good news is, savory smoothies lend themselves perfectly to meal prep. This section will provide you with the basics of meal prepping your savory smoothies.

Recipe: Kale and Bean Smoothie Prep Packs

Create your own smoothie prep packs by portioning out all your ingredients beforehand. For a kale and bean smoothie, portion out a handful of kale, half a can of white beans, a small cucumber, a spoonful of hemp seeds, and a pinch of salt in separate containers or ziplock bags. When you're ready to make your smoothie, just empty your pack into the blender, add water or broth, and blend until smooth.

Exploring International Flavors in Savory Smoothies

Savory smoothies offer a great platform to explore and experiment with flavors from around the world. This section will guide you through various international flavor profiles and how to incorporate them into your smoothies.

Recipe: Thai-Style Savory Smoothie

For a Thai-inspired savory smoothie, blend together a small cucumber, a small piece of fresh ginger, a handful of cilantro, a squeeze of lime juice, a spoonful of peanut butter, a pinch of chili flakes, and coconut water. The result is a refreshing smoothie that echoes the flavors of a Thai salad.

Pairing Your Savory Smoothies with Other Dishes

While savory smoothies can certainly be enjoyed on their own, sometimes it can be nice to pair them with other dishes. This section will provide you with some ideas on what to pair your savory smoothies with.

Recipe: Bell Pepper and Tomato Smoothie with Grilled Cheese

Blend together a red bell pepper, a ripe tomato, a small onion, a clove of garlic, a splash of red wine vinegar, and a drizzle of olive oil. Pair this smoothie with a classic grilled cheese sandwich for a comforting and balanced meal.

How to Make Your Savory Smoothies Look As Good As They Taste

We eat with our eyes first, so making your smoothies look good is just as important as making them taste good. This section will give you tips on how to make your savory smoothies look appealing, from choosing colorful ingredients to serving them in stylish glasses or bowls.

Recipe: Rainbow Vegetable Smoothie

To create a visually striking smoothie, select vegetables of different colors, such as a small beetroot, a carrot, a yellow bell pepper, a cucumber, and a handful of spinach. Blend each vegetable individually with a little water or broth, then layer them in a tall glass to create a rainbow effect.

Chapter 5

Sweet Treats: Dessert Smoothies That Won't Ruin Your Diet

Healthy dessert smoothies can offer the best of both worlds: the delicious flavors of your favorite sweets and the nutritional benefits of fruits and other healthful ingredients. But crafting a dessert smoothie that's both satisfying and diet-friendly requires some careful consideration. In this section, we'll look at the building blocks of healthy dessert smoothies, from choosing the right fruits to adding a natural sweetness.

Recipe: Strawberry Cheesecake Smoothie

To make a strawberry cheesecake smoothie, blend together a cup of fresh strawberries, half a cup of low-fat Greek yogurt, a spoonful of low-fat cream cheese, a spoonful of honey, a dash of vanilla extract, and a few ice cubes. The result is a creamy, sweet smoothie that tastes just like a strawberry cheesecake but is significantly lower in calories and fat.

Navigating the Sugar Trap in Dessert Smoothies

While fruits are a key ingredient in dessert smoothies, it's crucial to be mindful of their sugar content. This section will provide you with strategies to navigate the sugar trap in dessert smoothies, such as portion control, selecting fruits with lower sugar content, and using natural sweeteners sparingly.

Recipe: Low-Sugar Berry and Spinach Smoothie

For a low-sugar dessert smoothie, blend together a small handful of mixed berries, a handful of spinach, a spoonful of chia seeds, a spoonful of almond butter, a splash of almond milk, and a few drops of stevia. The berries and spinach provide natural sweetness and nutrients, while the chia seeds and almond butter add a satisfying creaminess.

Boosting the Nutritional Value of Your Dessert Smoothies

There are numerous ways to boost the nutritional value of your dessert smoothies, from adding protein-rich ingredients like Greek yogurt and protein powder to including fiber-rich ones like oats and flaxseeds. This section will provide you with tips and tricks to make your dessert smoothies not just tasty, but also nutritionally balanced.

Recipe: Chocolate Protein Smoothie

For a protein-packed dessert smoothie, blend together a banana, a spoonful of unsweetened cocoa powder, a spoonful of protein powder, a spoonful of peanut butter, and almond milk. This smoothie not only satisfies your chocolate cravings but also provides a good dose of protein to keep you satiated.

Experimenting with Superfood Dessert Smoothies

Superfoods like chia seeds, flaxseeds, and spirulina can add an extra boost of nutrition to your dessert smoothies. This section will explore different superfoods and how to incorporate them into your dessert smoothies for maximum health benefits.

Recipe: Superfood Blueberry and Spinach Smoothie

For a superfood dessert smoothie, blend together a handful of blueberries, a handful of spinach, a spoonful of chia seeds, a spoonful of honey, and almond milk. The blueberries and spinach provide antioxidants, while the chia seeds add fiber and omega-3 fatty acids.

Satisfying Specific Cravings with Dessert Smoothies

Whether you're craving chocolate, something fruity, or a classic dessert like apple pie or cheesecake, you can satisfy your specific cravings with a dessert smoothie. This section will provide you with ideas and recipes for different craving-inspired dessert smoothies.

Recipe: Apple Pie Smoothie

To satisfy an apple pie craving, blend together a small apple, a spoonful of oats, a dash of cinnamon, a spoonful of honey, a spoonful of Greek yogurt, and a splash of almond milk. This smoothie tastes remarkably similar to apple pie, but is much healthier and lower in calories.

Integrating Superfoods into Dessert Smoothies

Integrating superfoods into your dessert smoothies not only enhances their nutritional profile but can also help create unique and enticing flavor combinations. We'll discuss how to use these nutrient-dense foods, from exotic powders to seeds and nuts, to elevate the health benefits of your smoothie recipes.

Recipe: Mango and Turmeric Smoothie

For a tropical dessert smoothie with a superfood twist, blend together a ripe mango, a small banana, a spoonful of honey, a cup of almond milk, and a teaspoon of turmeric. The mango provides a sweet and tangy flavor, while the turmeric adds a hint of earthiness and a multitude of health benefits, including anti-inflammatory properties.

Creating Creamy Dessert Smoothies Without Dairy

For those who are lactose intolerant or choose to follow a dairy-free diet, finding ways to achieve the creamy texture typically provided by milk or yogurt can be a challenge. This section will explore dairy-free alternatives that can help you create creamy, satisfying dessert smoothies.

Recipe: Creamy Chocolate Avocado Smoothie

To make a creamy chocolate avocado smoothie, blend together a ripe avocado, a spoonful of unsweetened cocoa powder, a spoonful of honey, a dash of vanilla extract, and a cup of almond milk. The avocado provides a rich, creamy texture, while the cocoa powder satisfies your chocolate cravings.

Green Smoothie Revolution

Exploring Sweet and Savory Flavor Combinations in Dessert Smoothies

While dessert smoothies are traditionally sweet, there's no rule saying you can't add savory or spicy elements to them. This section will inspire you to experiment with unexpected flavor combinations in your dessert smoothies.

Recipe: Sweet and Spicy Pineapple and Cayenne Smoothie

For a dessert smoothie that balances sweetness with a hint of spice, blend together a cup of pineapple chunks, a small piece of fresh ginger, a spoonful of honey, a cup of coconut milk, and a pinch of cayenne pepper. The pineapple and ginger provide natural sweetness, while the cayenne pepper adds a kick that contrasts beautifully with the other flavors.

Utilizing Fresh Versus Frozen Fruits in Dessert Smoothies

The choice between fresh and frozen fruits can affect the texture and temperature of your dessert smoothies. This section will discuss the pros and cons of both, and provide guidance on when to use each.

Recipe: Fresh Peach and Yogurt Smoothie

To make a fresh peach and yogurt smoothie, blend together a ripe peach, half a cup of low-fat Greek yogurt, a spoonful of honey, and a few ice cubes. The fresh peach provides a natural sweetness and a slightly chunky texture, while the Greek yogurt adds creaminess.

The Art of Smoothie Bowl Making

Smoothie bowls offer a fun and creative alternative to traditional smoothies. This section will introduce you to the art of smoothie bowl making, from creating a thick smoothie base to decorating with an array of colorful toppings.

Recipe: Berry and Granola Smoothie Bowl

To make a berry and granola smoothie bowl, blend together a small banana, a handful of mixed berries, a spoonful of Greek yogurt, and a splash of almond milk until thick. Pour the smoothie into a bowl, and decorate with a handful of granola, a few fresh berries, and a drizzle of honey.

From understanding the foundations of making diet-friendly dessert smoothies, exploring various ways to enhance nutritional value, to trying out adventurous flavor profiles, we have spanned a wide spectrum of the dessert smoothie world. Equipped with this knowledge, you are well-prepared to create a variety of healthy, fulfilling, and flavorful dessert smoothies.

Elevating Your Smoothie Experience with Texture

One aspect of making enjoyable dessert smoothies that's often overlooked is texture. A smoothie can have the perfect balance of flavors, but if its texture is off, it might not be as enjoyable as it could be. In this section, we'll discuss how you can manipulate texture in your smoothies to create a more fulfilling and enjoyable eating experience.

Recipe: Raspberry Chia Seed Pudding Smoothie

To make a Raspberry Chia Seed Pudding Smoothie, start by preparing the chia pudding. Combine two tablespoons of chia seeds with half a cup of almond milk, and let it sit in the fridge for a few hours or overnight until it forms a gel-like consistency. Blend a cup of raspberries with half a cup of almond milk and a spoonful of honey. Pour the smoothie into a glass, then top it with the chia pudding. The chia pudding adds an interesting texture to the smoothie, making it feel more like a dessert.

Dessert Smoothies for Special Dietary Needs

Having dietary restrictions shouldn't mean you can't enjoy a tasty dessert smoothie. Whether you're vegan, gluten-free, or watching your sugar intake, there are plenty of ways to adapt smoothie recipes to fit your dietary needs.

Recipe: Vegan Banana and Almond Butter Smoothie

For a vegan dessert smoothie, blend together a ripe banana, two spoonfuls of almond butter, a cup of almond milk, a dash of cinnamon, and a spoonful of agave nectar. The almond butter and banana provide a creamy texture and natural sweetness, while the cinnamon and agave nectar add a hint of spice and additional sweetness.

Decorating Your Dessert Smoothies

Just as important as the taste of your dessert smoothie is its presentation. In this section, we'll discuss how you can use various toppings and garnishes to make your dessert smoothies look as good as they taste.

Recipe: Tropical Fruit Smoothie with Toasted Coconut

For a Tropical Fruit Smoothie with Toasted Coconut, blend together a cup of mixed tropical fruits (like pineapple, mango, and kiwi), a cup of coconut milk, and a spoonful of honey. Pour the smoothie into a glass, and top it with a sprinkle of toasted coconut flakes. The toasted coconut adds a delightful crunch and a burst of flavor that complements the tropical fruits.

Creating Seasonal Dessert Smoothies

Harnessing the flavors of the season can make your dessert smoothies even more enjoyable. From the freshness of summer berries to the comforting spices of fall, each season offers a unique palette of flavors to work with.

Recipe: Fall Spice Pumpkin Smoothie

To make a Fall Spice Pumpkin Smoothie, blend together half a cup of canned pumpkin puree, half a cup of Greek yogurt, a cup of almond milk, a spoonful of honey, and a dash each of cinnamon, nutmeg, and ginger. This smoothie is like a slice of pumpkin pie in a glass, making it the perfect dessert smoothie for a chilly fall day.
Incorporating Protein-Packed Ingredients in Your Smoothies

Protein is an essential nutrient that helps to keep you full and satisfied, which makes it a crucial component for dessert smoothies, especially for those looking to manage their weight. This section will explore different ways to incorporate protein-rich ingredients into your smoothies without compromising on taste.

Recipe: High-Protein Peanut Butter and Banana Smoothie

To make a High-Protein Peanut Butter and Banana Smoothie, blend together a ripe banana, two spoonfuls of natural peanut butter, a cup of unsweetened almond milk, a scoop of vanilla protein powder, and a spoonful of honey. The peanut butter and protein powder provide a substantial amount of protein, helping to keep you satisfied long after your dessert smoothie is gone.

Turning Your Smoothies into Frozen Treats

If you're looking for a frozen treat that's healthier than traditional ice cream, look no further than your smoothie ingredients. This section will teach you how to turn your favorite smoothie recipes into refreshing frozen desserts.

Recipe: Mixed Berry Smoothie Popsicles

To make Mixed Berry Smoothie Popsicles, blend together a cup of mixed berries, half a cup of Greek yogurt, a splash of almond milk, and a spoonful of honey. Pour the mixture into popsicle molds and freeze until solid. These smoothie popsicles are a healthier alternative to store-bought frozen treats and are perfect for a hot summer day.

Creating Dessert Smoothies for Kids

Getting kids to eat healthily can be a struggle, especially when it comes to desserts. This section will offer strategies and recipes for creating dessert smoothies that are not only nutritious but also kid-approved.

Recipe: Kid-Friendly Chocolate and Banana Smoothie

To make a Kid-Friendly Chocolate and Banana Smoothie, blend together a ripe banana, a spoonful of unsweetened cocoa powder, a cup of milk, and a spoonful of honey. This smoothie tastes like a chocolate milkshake but is packed with nutrients, making it a win-win for both parents and kids.

Achieving the Perfect Smoothie Consistency

The consistency of your smoothie plays a crucial role in how enjoyable it is to drink. Whether you prefer your smoothies thick and creamy or light and sippable, this section will offer tips on how to achieve your ideal smoothie consistency.

Recipe: Thick and Creamy Strawberry Smoothie

To make a Thick and Creamy Strawberry Smoothie, blend together a cup of frozen strawberries, half a cup of Greek yogurt, half a cup of almond milk, and a spoonful of honey. The frozen strawberries and Greek yogurt help to create a thick, creamy texture that's perfect for those who prefer a more substantial smoothie.

With all these tips, tricks, and recipes in your arsenal, you're ready to start creating a wide variety of dessert smoothies that won't ruin your diet. From protein-packed smoothies to kid-friendly options, there's a healthy dessert smoothie to satisfy every craving. So don't wait any longer – start blending and enjoy!

The world of chocolate smoothies offers endless possibilities for chocolate lovers. Decadent chocolate smoothie recipes can use cocoa powder, chocolate protein powder or chocolate syrup as the base. Try a chocolate peanut butter banana smoothie with cocoa powder, banana, peanut butter and milk. A mint chocolate smoothie made with cocoa powder, mint leaves, milk and honey is refreshing. Hazelnut butter paired with cocoa powder, bananas and milk makes for a delightful chocolate hazelnut smoothie. Don't forget about chocolate protein smoothies - simply blend a banana with chocolate protein powder, almond milk and you have a protein-packed treat. And for an ultra-indulgent chocolate brownie smoothie, blend cocoa powder, Greek yogurt, chocolate syrup and milk.

While chocolate smoothies are indulgent by nature, there are ways to lighten them up if you prefer a healthier option. Using plant-based milks like almond or oat milk instead of dairy can help reduce calories.

Sweetening with zero-calorie options like stevia instead of sugar also cuts some calories. You can boost nutrition by adding spinach, kale or avocado to your chocolate smoothie. Using dark chocolate or cacao powder is lower in sugar than milk chocolate. And replacing some of the cocoa powder with carob powder adds great chocolatey flavor while avoiding caffeine.

Don't limit yourself to basic chocolate smoothie recipes - get creative with unique flavor combinations! A chocolate-cherry smoothie pairs the sweet chocolate with tart cherry juice for a delicious contrast. Add a warming hint of spice to a chocolate smoothie with cinnamon. Coconut milk makes a chocolate smoothie rich and tropical. Kick up your chocolate intensity with a touch of cayenne in a Mexican chocolate smoothie. The sweet-tart blend of chocolate and raspberry is heavenly. Pumpkin puree can make for an ideal seasonal fall chocolate smoothie. And you can't go wrong blending chocolate with classic flavors like peanut butter and banana.

For an even more decadent way to enjoy chocolate smoothies, try turning them into smoothie bowls. Toppings like cacao nibs, granola and fresh fruit take the experience to the next level. Try topping a chocolate banana smoothie with sliced banana, crunchy cacao nibs and toasted coconut. Or blend a peanut butter chocolate smoothie and top with chopped peanuts, granola and chocolate chips for a peanut butter cup inspired treat. Hazelnut butter and chocolate is perfect topped with whole hazelnuts, chocolate shavings and fresh strawberry slices. And a mint chocolate smoothie bowl is amazing finished with cacao nibs, fresh mint and raspberries.

While delicious, chocolate smoothies can also deliver a healthy dose of vitamins, minerals and antioxidants. You can amp up the nutritional value by adding ingredients like spinach for vitamin A, vitamin K and folate. Avocado blends in creamy richness along with heart-healthy fats, fiber and potassium. Chia seeds or flaxseeds add an extra dose of fiber, protein and omega-3 fatty acids. The protein, fiber and vitamin E in almond butter complement chocolate wonderfully. And the antioxidants and anti-inflammatory benefits of cherries make them a stellar addition to chocolate smoothies. Even using dark chocolate can add antioxidants like flavonoids. So go ahead, enjoy an indulgent chocolate smoothie without guilt, as long as you include some nutritious ingredients! With the right mix, it can be a downright healthy treat any time of day.

For coffee addicts, combining coffee flavor with delicious dessert smoothies is a match made in heaven. There are endless possibilities when crafting a caffeinated sweet treat. The simplest way to add coffee flavor to smoothies is by replacing some of the milk or water in a recipe with freshly brewed coffee. This works especially well in chocolate, caramel or mocha-flavored smoothies, and the small amount of caffeine provides an energizing effect. For a more pronounced coffee taste, coffee extracts and syrups are very effective. Just a teaspoon of coffee extract or tablespoon of coffee syrup can infuse a smoothie with rich, roasted coffee undertones without overpowering other ingredients. Flavored coffee syrups like caramel, hazelnut and vanilla open up even more flavor combinations.

Another strategy for getting coffee flavor into smoothies is to use a coffee-flavored protein powder as a base ingredient. The powder dissolves evenly, ensuring the coffee taste is distributed throughout the smoothie. Both whey and plant-based protein powders like pea protein come in delicious coffee varieties. Some tasty coffee smoothies to try include a coffee banana made with banana, coffee and milk blended with honey. An iced mocha smoothie can be created by blending cocoa powder, coffee syrup, milk and ice for a frosty treat. Mix caramel sauce with coffee, Greek yogurt and milk for a caramel coffee delight. Coffee and hazelnut combine wonderfully in a smoothie with bananas for added sweetness. And a vanilla frappe smoothie is scrumptious blended from coffee extract, milk, vanilla protein powder and ice.

For the true coffee connoisseur, consider making your own coffee syrup or liqueur to take smoothie flavors to the next level. Simply infuse sugar syrup or alcohol with coffee beans for several hours or days depending on your desired intensity of flavor. Get creative with flavored versions like vanilla bean coffee syrup too. The possibilities are endless when you make your own artisanal coffee-flavored ingredients to mix into smoothies!

Oats are most often thought of as a breakfast food, but they can also add great texture, flavor and nutrition to smoothies that feel like a decadent dessert! The fiber in oats helps stabilize blood sugar for sustained energy, making them an ideal addition to sweet smoothie recipes. Old-fashioned or quick oats work best, as instant oats can turn mushy in smoothies. Try soaking oats in milk ahead of time to achieve a richer, creamier texture after blending. A couple tablespoons of dry oats per smoothie is perfect - too much can make it overly thick. For overnight oats, the refrigeration time allows the oats to absorb moisture and soften for at least 2 hours before blending. Substitute oat milk for dairy milk to get an extra oat flavor boost. And you can always sprinkle extra oats on top of smoothie bowls as a fun crunchy topping.

Some delicious oat-based smoothies to try include an apple pie oatmeal smoothie using oats, apple, cinnamon and almond milk. Carrots, Greek yogurt and cinnamon paired with oats creates a tasty carrot cake smoothie. Peanut butter and bananas taste great blended with oats and milk for a PB&J smoothie. Oats, pumpkin puree, Greek yogurt and fall spices like cinnamon and nutmeg make for an amazing pumpkin pie smoothie. And banana, almond butter and cinnamon blended with oats and milk evokes the flavor of banana bread. The bottom line is oats can enhance texture, flavor and nutrition in all kinds of smoothies, both fruity and decadent dessert-inspired ones. Feel free to get creative and come up with your own signature oat smoothie recipes!

One challenge of keeping dessert smoothies healthy is they often lack protein, which can lead to energy crashes later. The solution is to pack them with protein! Greek yogurt is an obvious protein-packed addition that also blends in creamy richness. Just mixing a few spoonfuls into a smoothie can provide 10-20 grams of protein. Cottage cheese is an unsung hero with around 13 grams of protein per half cup serving, and its mild flavor works well in many smoothies. Protein powders like whey and plant-based proteins from peas, hemp and more are easy ways to add a big protein punch, with 10-30 grams per scoop generally. Nut and seed butters like almond butter, peanut butter and sunflower seed butter not only provide protein but also healthy fats and creaminess. Chia and hemp seeds are great to sprinkle into smoothies for extra plant-based protein, fiber and omega-3 fatty acids. Even shelled edamame can be blended into fruity smoothies to sneak more protein in.

Some protein-packed smoothie recipes to try include a chocolate peanut butter banana smoothie made with cocoa powder, banana, peanut butter, milk and whey protein powder. Berries, cottage cheese, Greek yogurt and vanilla protein powder makes for a deliciously nutritious berry cheesecake smoothie. Pineapple, coconut milk, a dash of rum extract and hemp seeds can transport you to the tropics with a pina colada smoothie. Pumpkin spice smoothies are amazing with pumpkin, almond butter, cinnamon and whey protein. With a little creativity, you really can have both dessert and protein all in one convenient and delicious smoothie.

For lovers of bubble tea, also known as boba tea, much of the satisfaction comes from those fun, chewy tapioca pearls at the bottom of the cup. The good news is you can recreate this texture at home in smoothies with just a few simple additions. By far the most authentic option is to prepare your own tapioca pearls, which are essentially little juice-filled tapioca balls. You simply bring a pot of water to a boil, then add the tapioca pearls and simmer until they become translucent, about 15 minutes. Drain, then add them to your smoothie for that distinctive chewy boba texture. Another hack is using tapioca starch or flour, which can create a thick, pleasantly chewy texture when blended into smoothies containing milk or fruit juice. The starch particles plump up as they hydrate and absorb the surrounding liquid.

Chia seeds are another great way to mimic tapioca pearls, as they develop a gel-like coating when soaked in milk or juice. For best results, stir chia seeds into the liquid portion of your smoothie recipe and refrigerate for at least 15 minutes before blending, allowing time for that gel coating to form. And don't forget about fun toppings to finish your fruity boba-style smoothie! Popped boba, jelly cubes, mini mochi balls and lychee fruit make amazing smoothie add-ins. Some delicious fruity boba tea smoothies to try include a strawberry green tea smoothie with lychee jelly, a mango passionfruit smoothie with chia seeds, and a pineapple smoothie with coconut milk topped with cantaloupe cubes. The possibilities are endless when you embrace the bubble tea theme.

Smoothies make for a quick, nutritious breakfast or snack, but sometimes you need an extra dose of energy. Luckily there are many great mix-ins that can give your smoothies a power-up. Coffee and espresso are perfect for providing a midday pick-me-up, whether you add a splash of freshly brewed coffee or a teaspoon of instant espresso powder. Matcha, which is finely ground green tea leaves, provides caffeine plus antioxidant benefits - start with just 1 teaspoon per smoothie. Yerba mate is an herbal tea made from a South American plant that contains a unique form of caffeine. Try using 2-3 teaspoons of loose leaf yerba mate or a couple tea bags in your smoothies. Guarana powder is made from an Amazonian berry that's very high in caffeine, so use sparingly - just 1/4 to 1/2 teaspoon mixed into a smoothie. Another classic energy booster is ginseng - add 1-2 teaspoons of powdered ginseng root per smoothie for an extra lift. Maca powder, made from a Peruvian root vegetable, is also linked to sustained energy, stamina and mood; stir in 1 teaspoon or more. And for a natural lift, cacao powder provides energizing compounds like theobromine - try 2 tablespoons raw cacao powder. Chia seeds and flax seeds also promote alertness thanks to their omega-3 fatty acids - 2-3 teaspoons does the trick. With any energizing add-ins, moderation is key - don't overdo the caffeine! But adding one can give you the power to conquer that post-lunch energy slump.

Pre-workout smoothies are great for energizing your body with nutrients before exercise. But plain old fruit and protein smoothies can get boring. Why not create pre-workout smoothies that also taste like DESSERT? For a chocolate cherry smoothie, blend cocoa powder, cherries, banana, protein powder and almond milk. Strawberries, vanilla protein powder, almond milk and oats makes for a strawberry shortcake flavored smoothie. Peanut butter, banana, chocolate protein powder and milk comes together for a peanut butter cup smoothie. For carrot cake flavor, blend carrots, vanilla protein powder, cinnamon, walnuts, Greek yogurt and milk. Canned pumpkin, vanilla protein powder, cinnamon and almond milk evokes pumpkin pie. Banana bread flavors shine through in a smoothie with banana, almond butter, cinnamon, whey protein and almond milk. And blueberries, vanilla protein powder, almond milk and oats taste just like blueberry cobbler.

The key is to use healthy ingredients like fruit, protein powder, nut butters, Greek yogurt and oats as your base, then get creative with "dessert" flavors using cinnamon, vanilla, cocoa powder, etc. These tasty, tempting pre-workout smoothies make it easy to fuel up for the gym or any other exercise. They provide the perfect balance of energy, nutrition and indulgence you need to power through even your toughest workouts.

When craving something sweet and delicious, green smoothies might not immediately come to mind. But it is possible to create smoothies that taste decadent while also packing in leafy greens. The key is to disguise the veggies well so you barely taste them. Use milder greens like spinach and romaine lettuce, and start with just a handful - too much volume can create grassy or bitter flavors. Up the sweetness to mask greens by adding extra ripe, sweet fruit like mango, pineapple or banana. Liquid sweeteners like honey, maple syrup or pitted dates also help overwhelm any residual bitterness. Extracts like vanilla and almond add fragrant sweetness too. Stronger flavors like cocoa powder, peanut butter, coffee and pumpkin puree are also great to distract from and overpower the taste of veggies. And focusing on achieving a smooth, creamy texture with ingredients like Greek yogurt, avocado and nut butters helps the greens seamlessly blend into the background.

Some green smoothies that could pass for dessert include a chocolate peanut butter banana smoothie with a handful of spinach, which hides undetectably. A pumpkin pie smoothie tastes perfectly seasonal and decadent with kale and pumpkin pie spice mixed in. Romaine lettuce complements the flavors of strawberry and vanilla for a strawberry cheesecake smoothie. Carrot cake flavors shine through despite the greens when you blend carrots, pineapple, cinnamon and spinach. Basil complements chocolate and cherry beautifully in a smoothie with cocoa powder. And a tropical piña colada smoothie still tastes refreshing with a handful of spinach. With the right balance of flavors and textures, you can "hide" veggies in your dessert smoothies and get all the nutritional benefits - but it will just taste sweet and delicious going down!

Probiotics are beneficial gut bacteria that support digestive and overall health, and smoothies can be great vehicles for getting more of them. There are many tasty ways to add a probiotic boost: Greek yogurt provides billions of live and active cultures, so use a couple spoonfuls of plain unsweetened varieties. Kefir is a tangy, drinkable form of yogurt absolutely loaded with probiotics. Use it plain or choose from the many available fruit flavors. Fermented kombucha tea offers probiotics too, but flavors can vary widely, so start with unflavored or lighter options like ginger or berry flavors. Even just a spoonful of the juice from sauerkraut, kimchi or other fermented vegetables adds a dose of probiotics without overpowering smoothies. Just a few bites of pickled carrots, beets, cauliflower or cucumbers blended in does the trick. And don't forget prebiotic foods - fibers that feed probiotics and enhance their effectiveness. Great prebiotic options are banana, blueberry, asparagus and oats.

Some tasty probiotic smoothie recipes to try include a classic strawberry smoothie with Greek yogurt, strawberries, banana and milk. Piña colada flavors come through in a smoothie with pineapple, coconut milk and plain kefir. For a green smoothie, blend kale, green apple, kimchi juice and Greek yogurt. Beets, blueberries, plain kombucha, banana and ginger make a stellar beet berry probiotic smoothie. Dessert smoothies are ideal for hiding small amounts of fermented add-ins and providing enough sweetness to mask any sourness. Focus on fruits and flavors that complement the mild fermented tastes. Just a spoonful or two is all it takes to give your gut health an extra boost with smoothies.

When cooler fall and winter weather arrives, warm spices like cinnamon, nutmeg, ginger and cloves add cozy flavor to smoothies and evoke classic fall and winter desserts. Cinnamon enhances apple, pear, carrot and sweet potato smoothies, making them reminiscent of apple pie, carrot cake or gingerbread. Nutmeg complements pumpkin, banana, vanilla and cocoa smoothies, giving them a flavor similar to eggnog or pumpkin pie. Ginger adds comforting zip to pear, apple, carrot and pumpkin smoothies. Cloves provide a lovely accent and fragrance to apple cider and orange smoothies, also pairing wonderfully with chocolate. Allspice gives great background flavor to smoothies made with pumpkin, pear or peach. And cardamom adds wonderful aroma to cherry, fig or persimmon smoothies, making them taste indulgent.

Some enticing spice-infused smoothies to try are a pumpkin pie smoothie with pumpkin puree, Greek yogurt, nutmeg and cinnamon. Apple, cinnamon, nutmeg and Greek yogurt blended together taste just like apple cider donuts. Banana, molasses, ginger, cinnamon and cloves creates a smoothie reminiscent of gingerbread cookies. For Mexican hot chocolate flavors, blend cocoa powder, cinnamon and a touch of cayenne. And chai tea comes through in a smoothie with black tea, almond milk, cardamom, ginger and cloves. Feel free to get creative with combinations of seasonal produce and fragrant spices that evoke cozy desserts! The possibilities are nearly endless for cool weather smoothies that warm you from the inside out.

Why choose between a smoothie and dessert when you can combine them into one tasty blended treat? There are so many creative smoothie options inspired by classic dessert flavors. For apple pie in a glass, blend apples, cinnamon, nutmeg, Greek yogurt and oats. Pumpkin pie flavors shine through in a smoothie with pumpkin puree, Greek yogurt, cinnamon and nutmeg. Carrot cake flavors emerge when you blend carrots, Greek yogurt, cinnamon and walnuts.

Mendocino Brock

Chapter 6

Nutrient Powerhouses: Antioxidant and Superfood Smoothies

The term 'superfood' might sound like a marketing gimmick, but it is used to classify certain foods that are extremely nutrient-dense, meaning they are rich in vitamins, minerals, antioxidants, fiber, and other beneficial compounds. Incorporating these superfoods into your diet can enhance your health in numerous ways. This chapter aims to guide you in creating antioxidant-rich and superfood smoothies, providing you with potent nutrient powerhouses in each sip.

Understanding Antioxidants and Their Importance

Antioxidants are compounds that help defend your cells from damage caused by potentially harmful molecules known as free radicals. Consuming a diet rich in antioxidants may help increase your blood antioxidant levels to fight oxidative stress and reduce the risk of chronic diseases.

Recipe: Blueberry and Spinach Antioxidant Smoothie

Blueberries and spinach are both known for their high antioxidant content. To make a Blueberry and Spinach Antioxidant Smoothie, blend together a cup of blueberries, a handful of spinach, a ripe banana for natural sweetness, a cup of almond milk, and a spoonful of chia seeds. This smoothie is a true antioxidant powerhouse, packed with vitamins and minerals, fiber, and heart-healthy omega-3 fats from the chia seeds.

An Introduction to Superfoods

Superfoods is a term used to describe foods that are nutrient-dense and thus considered particularly good for one's health. Some popular examples of superfoods include kale, spinach, berries, avocados, nuts and seeds, and many others. Incorporating these into your smoothies is an easy way to reap their health benefits.

Recipe: Green Superfood Smoothie

For a Green Superfood Smoothie, blend together a handful of kale, a cup of pineapple chunks, half an avocado, a cup of coconut water, and a spoonful of spirulina powder. Kale provides a hefty dose of vitamins A, C, and K, while avocado adds healthy fats, fiber, and creaminess to the smoothie. Pineapple gives it a tropical flavor and additional vitamin C, and spirulina powder offers a protein boost along with a wide range of other nutrients.

Superfoods for Specific Health Benefits

Different superfoods offer different health benefits, ranging from boosting your immune system to improving digestion, from enhancing skin health to increasing energy levels. Understanding these benefits can help you select the superfoods that best suit your specific health needs.

Recipe: Digestion-Boosting Smoothie

To make a Digestion-Boosting Smoothie, blend together a cup of papaya chunks, a spoonful of ginger, a cup of kefir, and a spoonful of honey. Papaya is rich in an enzyme called papain, which aids digestion, and ginger has long been known for its digestive benefits. Kefir is a fermented dairy product packed with probiotics, which are beneficial for gut health.

Boosting Your Smoothie with Antioxidant-Rich Spices

Spices are not only valuable for adding flavor to your smoothies, but many also have potent antioxidant properties. Turmeric, cinnamon, and cacao are among the spices that can boost the antioxidant content of your smoothies.

Recipe: Anti-Inflammatory Turmeric and Mango Smoothie

Green Smoothie Revolution

To make an Anti-Inflammatory Turmeric and Mango Smoothie, blend together a cup of mango chunks, a spoonful of turmeric, a cup of almond milk, a spoonful of chia seeds, and a touch of black pepper. The black pepper enhances the absorption of curcumin, the active ingredient in turmeric known for its anti-inflammatory and antioxidant properties.

Creating Antioxidant and Superfood Smoothie Bowls

Smoothie bowls are a popular way to enjoy your nutrient-packed smoothies with a spoon, allowing for an array of tasty and nutritious toppings. They offer an opportunity to add even more superfoods to your meal.

Recipe: Acai Berry Smoothie Bowl

To make an Acai Berry Smoothie Bowl, blend together an acai berry packet, a ripe banana, a splash of almond milk, and a spoonful of honey. Pour the smoothie into a bowl and top it with sliced bananas, fresh berries, granola, and a drizzle of honey. Acai berries are rich in antioxidants, fiber, and heart-healthy fats, making them a worthy superfood to feature in your smoothie bowl.

Maximizing Nutrient Absorption

While it's important to consume nutrient-dense foods, it's equally vital to optimize their absorption. Certain nutrients are better absorbed when eaten in combination with others, and this section will provide you with the information you need to make the most of your antioxidant and superfood smoothies.

Recipe: Vitamin C Boosting Smoothie

Vitamin C helps enhance the absorption of iron, particularly the type of iron found in plant-based foods. To make a Vitamin C Boosting Smoothie, blend together a handful of spinach (rich in plant-based iron), a cup of strawberries (packed with vitamin C), a ripe banana, and a cup of almond milk. This smoothie will not only provide you with iron and vitamin C, but also fiber and other beneficial nutrients.

Supercharging Your Smoothies with Seeds

Seeds like flaxseeds, chia seeds, and hemp seeds are considered superfoods because of their rich nutrient content. They provide healthy fats, fiber, protein, and various vitamins and minerals. Adding them to your smoothies can significantly boost their nutritional value.

Recipe: Omega-3 Rich Smoothie

Omega-3 fatty acids are essential fats that have numerous health benefits. To make an Omega-3 Rich Smoothie, blend together a cup of blueberries, a ripe banana, a cup of almond milk, and a spoonful each of chia seeds, flaxseeds, and hemp seeds. All three seeds are excellent sources of plant-based omega-3s.

Catering to Dietary Restrictions and Preferences

Whether you're vegan, lactose intolerant, gluten-free, or simply prefer plant-based foods, you can still enjoy nutrient-packed smoothies. This section will offer tips and recipes for creating antioxidant and superfood smoothies that cater to various dietary restrictions and preferences.

Recipe: Vegan Superfood Smoothie

To make a Vegan Superfood Smoothie, blend together a handful of kale, a cup of mixed berries, half an avocado, a cup of almond milk, and a spoonful of spirulina powder. This smoothie is 100% plant-based and filled with a wide range of nutrients.

Including Superfoods in Your Diet Beyond Smoothies

While this book focuses on smoothies, superfoods can and should be incorporated into other meals as well. This section will offer suggestions for how to include more superfoods in your everyday diet.

Recipe: Superfood Salad

For a Superfood Salad, combine a handful of kale, a handful of spinach, half an avocado (sliced), a small handful of almonds, and a small handful of blueberries. Dress it with a vinaigrette made from olive oil, apple cider vinegar, honey, and a pinch each of salt and pepper. This salad is bursting with antioxidants, healthy fats, and other essential nutrients.

Smoothies for Specific Nutrient Needs

Every individual is unique in their nutrient needs. Whether you're an athlete requiring more protein, a pregnant woman needing extra iron, or a busy professional seeking an energy boost, there are antioxidant and superfood smoothie recipes that can help you meet those specific needs.

Recipe: High-Protein Superfood Smoothie

This High-Protein Superfood Smoothie uses a combination of plant and animal-based protein sources to provide a well-rounded amino acid profile. Blend together a scoop of your preferred protein powder, a spoonful of almond butter, a cup of Greek yogurt, a ripe banana, a handful of spinach, and a cup of almond milk. With this smoothie, you're getting protein from various sources, as well as a host of other beneficial nutrients.

Understanding Phytonutrients and Their Benefits

Phytonutrients are naturally occurring compounds in plants that are responsible for their color, smell, and taste. They also offer health benefits to those who consume them. By consuming a diverse array of colorful fruits and vegetables, you can ensure you're getting a broad range of these beneficial compounds.

Recipe: Rainbow Phytonutrient Smoothie

To make a Rainbow Phytonutrient Smoothie, blend together a handful of spinach, a few chunks each of pineapple, mango, and strawberries, and half a beetroot. Add a cup of coconut water for hydration and a spoonful of chia seeds for added fiber and omega-3s. This smoothie provides a range of phytonutrients thanks to the variety of colorful fruits and vegetables.

Smoothies for Immune Support

With the rich nutrient content of superfoods and the protective properties of antioxidants, it's no surprise that these smoothies can also help support your immune system.

Recipe: Immune-Boosting Smoothie

For an Immune-Boosting Smoothie, blend together a cup of orange segments, half a cup of strawberries, a handful of spinach, a spoonful of ginger, a spoonful of honey, and a cup of kefir. Oranges and strawberries provide vitamin C, spinach offers vitamin A, ginger has anti-inflammatory properties, honey soothes the throat, and kefir provides probiotics, all of which contribute to supporting the immune system.

Creating Creamy Smoothies without Dairy

For those avoiding dairy, there are many other ways to achieve the desired creaminess in your smoothies. From avocados to bananas to plant-based yogurts, this section will introduce you to various dairy-free methods to create creamy smoothies.

Recipe: Dairy-Free Creamy Avocado Smoothie

To make a Dairy-Free Creamy Avocado Smoothie, blend together half an avocado, a ripe banana, a spoonful of almond butter, a spoonful of honey, and a cup of almond milk. This smoothie is creamy and satisfying, yet completely dairy-free.
The Benefits of Organically Grown Ingredients

Organic foods are grown without the use of synthetic fertilizers and pesticides, which can leave residues on fruits and vegetables. Organic farming practices are designed to encourage soil and water conservation and reduce pollution. While organic produce can be slightly more expensive, it is a worthwhile investment for the potential health benefits and environmental sustainability.

Recipe: Organic Berry Blast Smoothie

For an Organic Berry Blast Smoothie, combine a cup of organic mixed berries, a ripe banana, a spoonful of organic almond butter, and a cup of organic almond milk. Enjoy the sweet and tangy flavors of this smoothie, while knowing that you're reducing your exposure to potentially harmful chemicals.

The Importance of Hydration

Hydration is an often overlooked component of health. While plain water is always a great choice, smoothies can also contribute to your daily fluid intake. Many fruits and vegetables have a high water content, and the addition of liquids like milk or coconut water also aids hydration.

Recipe: Hydrating Cucumber Melon Smoothie

To make a Hydrating Cucumber Melon Smoothie, blend together half a cucumber, a cup of honeydew melon, a few mint leaves, a spoonful of honey, and a cup of coconut water. This smoothie is incredibly refreshing and hydrating, making it perfect for hot summer days or after an intense workout.

Balancing Taste and Nutrition

While it's important for smoothies to be nutritious, they should also be delicious. After all, you're more likely to stick with a healthy habit if you actually enjoy it. This section will offer tips for balancing taste and nutrition in your smoothies.

Recipe: Perfectly Balanced Pineapple Kale Smoothie

For a Perfectly Balanced Pineapple Kale Smoothie, blend together a handful of kale, a cup of pineapple chunks, half an avocado, a spoonful of honey, and a cup of almond milk. Pineapple adds natural sweetness to balance the bitterness of kale, while avocado provides creaminess and healthy fats.

Smoothies for Skin Health

Many antioxidants and superfoods can support skin health. For example, vitamin C aids in collagen production, omega-3s can help reduce inflammation, and fiber can support gut health, which is linked to skin health.

Recipe: Glowing Skin Smoothie

To make a Glowing Skin Smoothie, combine a cup of orange segments, a handful of spinach, half an avocado, a spoonful of flaxseeds, and a cup of kefir. This smoothie is packed with nutrients that support skin health, and it tastes great too.

Maximizing Nutrient Absorption

Digestibility and absorption are important considerations when consuming any food, and smoothies are no exception. Some nutrients are better absorbed when consumed with certain other nutrients. For example, the fat-soluble vitamins A, D, E, and K are better absorbed when consumed with fat. Adding a source of healthy fat, like avocados or nuts, can therefore enhance the nutrient absorption of your smoothies.

Recipe: Nutrient-Boosting Mango Avocado Smoothie

For a Nutrient-Boosting Mango Avocado Smoothie, blend together a cup of mango chunks, half an avocado, a handful of spinach, a spoonful of chia seeds, and a cup of coconut milk. This smoothie provides a range of nutrients, and the healthy fats from the avocado and coconut milk help to enhance their absorption.

The Role of Fiber in Health

Dietary fiber plays many important roles in health, including supporting digestive health, maintaining blood sugar levels, and promoting feelings of fullness. Many fruits, vegetables, and grains that are commonly used in smoothies are excellent sources of fiber.

Recipe: High-Fiber Apple Oat Smoothie

To make a High-Fiber Apple Oat Smoothie, combine a chopped apple, a handful of spinach, a spoonful of almond butter, a quarter cup of rolled oats, and a cup of almond milk. This smoothie is high in fiber, helping to support digestive health and keep you feeling full.

Smoothies for Heart Health

Green Smoothie Revolution

Heart disease is a leading cause of death worldwide. Consuming a diet rich in fruits, vegetables, whole grains, lean proteins, and healthy fats can support heart health. Smoothies can be a convenient and delicious way to incorporate these heart-healthy foods into your diet.

Recipe: Heart-Healthy Berry Beet Smoothie

For a Heart-Healthy Berry Beet Smoothie, blend together a cup of mixed berries, half a cooked beet, a handful of spinach, a spoonful of flaxseeds, and a cup of kefir. This smoothie is packed with heart-healthy nutrients like fiber, omega-3s, and probiotics.

Choosing a High-Quality Blender

The tool you use to make your smoothies can also impact the final product. A high-quality blender can help achieve a smooth, creamy texture, even when blending tough ingredients like kale or nuts. Consider investing in a good blender to enhance your smoothie-making experience.The term 'superfood' might sound like a marketing gimmick, but it is used to classify certain foods that are extremely nutrient-dense, meaning they are rich in vitamins, minerals, antioxidants, fiber, and other beneficial compounds. Incorporating these superfoods into your diet can enhance your health in numerous ways. This chapter aims to guide you in creating antioxidant-rich and superfood smoothies, providing you with potent nutrient powerhouses in each sip.

Understanding Antioxidants and Their Importance. Antioxidants are compounds that help defend your cells from damage caused by potentially harmful molecules known as free radicals. Consuming a diet rich in antioxidants may help increase your blood antioxidant levels to fight oxidative stress and reduce the risk of chronic diseases. Blueberries and spinach are both known for their high antioxidant content. To make a Blueberry and Spinach Antioxidant Smoothie, blend together a cup of blueberries, a handful of spinach, a ripe banana for natural sweetness, a cup of almond milk, and a spoonful of chia seeds. This smoothie is a true antioxidant powerhouse, packed with vitamins and minerals, fiber, and heart-healthy omega-3 fats from the chia seeds.

An Introduction to Superfoods. Superfoods is a term used to describe foods that are nutrient-dense and thus considered particularly good for one's health. Some popular examples of superfoods include kale, spinach, berries, avocados, nuts and seeds, and many others. Incorporating these into your smoothies is an easy way to reap their health benefits. For a Green Superfood Smoothie, blend together a handful of kale, a cup of pineapple chunks, half an avocado, a cup of coconut water, and a spoonful of spirulina powder. Kale provides a hefty dose of vitamins A, C, and K, while avocado adds healthy fats, fiber, and creaminess to the smoothie. Pineapple gives it a tropical flavor and additional vitamin C, and spirulina powder offers a protein boost along with a wide range of other nutrients.

Superfoods for Specific Health Benefits. Different superfoods offer different health benefits, ranging from boosting your immune system to improving digestion, from enhancing skin health to increasing energy levels. Understanding these benefits can help you select the superfoods that best suit your specific health needs. To make a Digestion-Boosting Smoothie, blend together a cup of papaya chunks, a spoonful of ginger, a cup of kefir, and a spoonful of honey. Papaya is rich in an enzyme called papain, which aids digestion, and ginger has long been known for its digestive benefits. Kefir is a fermented dairy product packed with probiotics, which are beneficial for gut health. Other examples of superfoods that can aid digestion include: yogurt, which contains probiotics that support gut health - use plain, unsweetened yogurt; chia seeds, which are rich in soluble fiber that can act as a prebiotic to feed good gut bacteria; flaxseeds, another great source of soluble fiber to promote regularity; fennel, which contains anethole, a compound that helps relax gastrointestinal muscles; and aloe vera gel from aloe leaves which has anti-inflammatory properties that soothe the digestive tract.

Boosting Your Smoothie with Antioxidant-Rich Spices. Spices are not only valuable for adding flavor to your smoothies, but many also have potent antioxidant properties. Turmeric, cinnamon, and cacao are among the spices that can boost the antioxidant content of your smoothies. To make an Anti-Inflammatory Turmeric and Mango Smoothie, blend together a cup of mango chunks, a spoonful of turmeric, a cup of almond milk, a spoonful of chia seeds, and a touch of black pepper. The black pepper enhances the absorption of curcumin, the active ingredient in turmeric known for its anti-inflammatory and antioxidant properties. Other antioxidant-rich spices to try adding to smoothies include: cinnamon, which contains polyphenols that act as antioxidants and may also help regulate blood sugar; ginger, which contains gingerol, a compound with antioxidant and anti-inflammatory effects; clove, which is very high in antioxidants and provides a strong, spicy flavor; cacao powder, which is made from cacao beans and is rich in flavanols with antioxidant activity; and cardamom, which imparts subtle spice and is a source of antioxidants like quercetin.

Creating Antioxidant and Superfood Smoothie Bowls. Smoothie bowls are a popular way to enjoy your nutrient-packed smoothies with a spoon, allowing for an array of tasty and nutritious toppings. They offer an opportunity to add even more superfoods to your meal. To make an Acai Berry Smoothie Bowl, blend together an acai berry packet, a ripe banana, a splash of almond milk, and a spoonful of honey. Pour the smoothie into a bowl and top it with sliced bananas, fresh berries, granola, and a drizzle of honey. Acai berries are rich in antioxidants, fiber, and heart-healthy fats, making them a worthy superfood to feature in your smoothie bowl. Other delicious and nutrient-dense toppings for smoothie bowls include: sliced fruit like bananas, kiwi, mango, and berries which provide natural sweetness; nuts and seeds like walnuts, almonds, chia seeds, and hemp hearts which add protein and healthy fats; nut butter like almond, peanut, or cashew butter which adds creaminess and satisfaction; granola, but look for unsweetened varieties without added sugars; coconut flakes for texture and subtle coconut flavor; and cacao nibs which impart chocolatey flavor and antioxidants.

Maximizing Nutrient Absorption. While it's important to consume nutrient-dense foods, it's equally vital to optimize their absorption. Certain nutrients are better absorbed when eaten in combination with others, and this section will provide you with the information you need to make the most of your antioxidant and superfood smoothies. To make a Vitamin C Boosting Smoothie, blend together a handful of spinach (rich in plant-based iron), a cup of strawberries (packed with vitamin C), a ripe banana, and a cup of almond milk. This smoothie will not only provide you with iron and vitamin C, but also fiber and other beneficial nutrients. Here are some other nutrient combinations that can maximize absorption: fat soluble vitamins (A, D, E, K) require fat for absorption so add a source of healthy fats like avocado, nuts or nut butter; carotenoids like beta-carotene are better absorbed with some fat so pair carrots or sweet potatoes with almond milk; calcium absorption is aided by vitamin D so add a vitamin D-fortified milk or yogurt; iron is enhanced by vitamin C so combine iron-rich spinach with vitamin C-rich citrus; and magnesium requires calcium for optimal absorption so add yogurt or milk to greens.

Supercharging Your Smoothies with Seeds. Seeds like flaxseeds, chia seeds, and hemp seeds are considered superfoods because of their rich nutrient content. They provide healthy fats, fiber, protein, and various vitamins and minerals. Adding them to your smoothies can significantly boost their nutritional value. To make an Omega-3 Rich Smoothie, blend together a cup of blueberries, a ripe banana, a cup of almond milk, and a spoonful each of chia seeds, flaxseeds, and hemp seeds. All three seeds are excellent sources of plant-based omega-3s. Other nutrient-dense seeds to try adding to smoothies include: pumpkin seeds which are rich in zinc, iron, magnesium, and antioxidants; sunflower seeds, a great source of vitamin E, selenium, B vitamins; sesame seeds, high in calcium, copper, manganese, and healthy fats; poppy seeds which are tiny but nutritious, providing iron, zinc, fiber; and pomegranate seeds which are bursting with antioxidants like anthocyanins.

Catering to Dietary Restrictions and Preferences. Whether you're vegan, lactose intolerant, gluten-free, or simply prefer plant-based foods, you can still enjoy nutrient-packed smoothies. This section will offer tips and recipes for creating antioxidant and superfood smoothies that cater to various dietary restrictions and preferences. To make a Vegan Superfood Smoothie, blend together a handful of kale, a cup of mixed berries, half an avocado, a cup of almond milk, and a spoonful of spirulina powder. This smoothie is 100% plant-based and filled with a wide range of nutrients. Here are some substitutions to make smoothies suitable for different diets: for dairy-free use plant-based milks like almond, coconut, oat and avocado adds creaminess; for gluten-free opt for gluten-free oats, nuts, seeds instead of wheat grains; for vegan exchange dairy for plant-based milk and yogurt, eggs for chia or flax eggs; for keto focus on low carb ingredients like avocado, nut butters, chia seeds; for low sugar replace fruit with veggies like spinach, kale, cucumber.

In conclusion, understanding how to maximize the nutrient content and absorption of your smoothies can help you get the most out of this health habit. With the right knowledge and ingredients, you can create antioxidant and superfood smoothies that are not only delicious, but also deeply nourishing. As you experiment with different ingredients and combinations, remember that the ultimate goal is to nurture and nourish your body. Happy blending!

Mendocino Brock

Chapter 7

Detox and Cleanse: Smoothies for Purifying Your System

Detoxing and cleansing have been a part of human health practices for centuries. The idea is to consume certain types of foods to help your body's natural detoxification processes. It's important to note that the human body is naturally capable of detoxing itself through organs like the liver, kidneys, skin, and lungs. However, consuming certain foods can aid these natural processes.

Recipe: Citrus and Ginger Detox Smoothie

For a Citrus and Ginger Detox Smoothie, combine a cup of freshly squeezed orange juice, half a lemon's juice, a small piece of ginger, a handful of parsley, and a cup of water. Citrus fruits are known for their detoxifying properties due to their high vitamin C content, which supports the liver's function. Ginger aids digestion, and parsley has diuretic properties, which can help the body eliminate toxins.

Understanding the Role of Your Liver

Your liver is your body's main detox organ. It filters the blood coming from the digestive tract before it's passed to the rest of the body. It also detoxifies chemicals and metabolizes drugs. Certain foods and drinks can support liver health and its detoxification functions.

Recipe: Liver-Loving Beet and Berry Smoothie

For a Liver-Loving Beet and Berry Smoothie, blend together a cup of mixed berries, half a cooked beet, a handful of spinach, a spoonful of flaxseeds, and a cup of almond milk. Beets are known for their liver-supporting properties, as they can help to cleanse and detoxify the liver. Berries, spinach, and flaxseeds provide an array of antioxidants to support overall health.

The Importance of Hydration in Detox

Hydration plays a crucial role in detoxification. The body needs water to process and eliminate toxins. While drinking plain water is crucial, consuming high-water fruits and vegetables can also contribute to your hydration status.

Recipe: Hydrating Watermelon and Mint Smoothie

To make a Hydrating Watermelon and Mint Smoothie, combine two cups of watermelon chunks, a few fresh mint leaves, a squeeze of lime, and a cup of coconut water. Watermelon is over 90% water, making it a highly hydrating food. Mint and lime add refreshing flavors, and coconut water provides electrolytes.

The Power of Antioxidants in Detox

Antioxidants are molecules that help protect the body from harmful substances called free radicals. When the body has too many free radicals, it can lead to a state of oxidative stress, which can damage cells. Consuming foods high in antioxidants can help the body neutralize these free radicals.

Recipe: Antioxidant-Rich Berry and Acai Smoothie

For an Antioxidant-Rich Berry and Acai Smoothie, blend together a cup of mixed berries, an acai berry packet, a spoonful of chia seeds, and a cup of almond milk. Berries and acai are some of the highest antioxidant foods available. Chia seeds provide additional antioxidants and fiber.

How Fiber Supports Detox

Dietary fiber can support your body's natural detoxification processes in several ways. First, fiber can help regulate your bowels, which is one way your body eliminates waste and toxins. Second, some types of fiber can bind to toxins in the digestive tract and help remove them from the body.

Recipe: High-Fiber Apple and Flax Smoothie

To make a High-Fiber Apple and Flax Smoothie, combine a chopped apple, a handful of spinach, a spoonful of ground flaxseeds, a spoonful of chia seeds, and a cup of almond milk. Apples and flaxseeds are high in fiber, and spinach provides additional detox-supporting nutrients.

Probiotics and Detoxification

Probiotics play a significant role in maintaining our health by aiding digestion, absorption, and the production of essential vitamins. Some researchers also believe that probiotics might assist in detoxification. By enhancing gut health, they can help the body dispose of toxins and other harmful substances. Including probiotic-rich foods or supplements in your smoothies can enhance their detoxification potential.

Recipe: Probiotic-Rich Kefir and Berry Smoothie

For a Probiotic-Rich Kefir and Berry Smoothie, blend together a cup of mixed berries, a cup of kefir, a banana, and a spoonful of honey. Kefir is a fermented milk product that is rich in probiotics. Berries provide antioxidants, and the banana adds a creamy texture and additional nutrients.

Understanding Phytonutrients and Their Role in Detoxification

Phytonutrients, also known as phytochemicals, are chemicals produced by plants. They are found in fruits, vegetables, grains, beans, and other plants. Some phytonutrients are known for their antioxidant and anti-inflammatory benefits, both of which support the body's natural detoxification processes.

Recipe: Phytonutrient-Packed Spinach and Kiwi Smoothie

To make a Phytonutrient-Packed Spinach and Kiwi Smoothie, blend together a handful of spinach, two peeled kiwis, a banana, and a cup of coconut water. Spinach and kiwis are rich in various phytonutrients, and the banana adds a creamy texture and natural sweetness.

The Role of Protein in Detoxification

Protein plays a crucial role in detoxification. The liver, which is the body's main detox organ, requires amino acids from protein to perform its detoxification processes. Consuming enough protein is therefore important for optimal detoxification.

Recipe: Protein-Packed Almond and Banana Smoothie

For a Protein-Packed Almond and Banana Smoothie, blend together a banana, a spoonful of almond butter, a scoop of your favorite protein powder, and a cup of almond milk. This smoothie is high in protein, helping to support the liver's detoxification functions.

Detoxing and Weight Loss

While weight loss is not the primary goal of detoxing, consuming nutrient-dense and low-calorie smoothies can contribute to weight loss by creating a calorie deficit. However, it's important to note that sustainable weight loss involves a combination of balanced eating, regular exercise, and healthy lifestyle habits.

Recipe: Weight Loss-Friendly Green Detox Smoothie

To make a Weight Loss-Friendly Green Detox Smoothie, blend together a handful of kale, half a cucumber, a green apple, a squeeze of lemon, and a cup of water. This smoothie is low in calories and high in nutrients, supporting weight loss while also aiding detoxification.

Conclusion: Maintaining Balance in Detox

In conclusion, it's important to remember that detoxification is a natural process that your body carries out daily. While the idea of detoxing through diet can seem appealing, it's essential to maintain balance and not to rely solely on specific foods or drinks for detoxification.

Hydrate and Detoxify with Water-Based Smoothies

Green Smoothie Revolution

Hydration is an essential aspect of detoxification, as water helps to flush out toxins from the body. It's important to ensure that you're consuming enough water each day, and including water-rich ingredients in your smoothies can help with this. Cucumbers and watermelons are excellent examples of such ingredients due to their high water content.

Recipe: Hydrating Cucumber and Watermelon Smoothie

For a Hydrating Cucumber and Watermelon Smoothie, blend together half a cucumber, two cups of diced watermelon, a handful of fresh mint leaves, and a cup of coconut water. This smoothie is not only refreshing but also packed with hydrating ingredients that aid in detoxification.

The Importance of Fiber in Detoxification

Fiber plays a critical role in the body's detoxification process. It aids digestion and helps regulate the body's use of sugars, helping to keep hunger and blood sugar in check. Fiber also helps to bind and eliminate toxins from the body, hence the importance of including fiber-rich ingredients in your smoothies, like berries, bananas, and chia seeds.

Recipe: Fiber-Rich Blueberry and Banana Smoothie

To make a Fiber-Rich Blueberry and Banana Smoothie, blend together a cup of blueberries, a banana, a spoonful of chia seeds, and a cup of almond milk. This smoothie is packed with fiber, helping to support your body's natural detox processes.

Smoothies with Anti-inflammatory Ingredients

Chronic inflammation in the body can lead to various health issues, including heart disease, cancer, and autoimmune diseases. Certain foods, however, are known for their anti-inflammatory properties, such as turmeric, ginger, and berries, and including these in your smoothies can help to fight inflammation.

Recipe: Anti-inflammatory Turmeric and Ginger Smoothie

To make an Anti-inflammatory Turmeric and Ginger Smoothie, blend together a small piece of fresh turmeric, a small piece of fresh ginger, a cup of pineapple chunks, a banana, and a cup of coconut milk. This smoothie is rich in anti-inflammatory ingredients, which can support your body's detoxification processes by reducing inflammation.

The Importance of Healthy Fats in Detoxification

Healthy fats are essential for optimal health, and they can also aid in detoxification. They help the body absorb certain nutrients and produce hormones. Avocado, flaxseeds, and chia seeds are examples of ingredients rich in healthy fats that can be included in your detox smoothies.

Recipe: Healthy Fat-Packed Avocado and Flaxseed Smoothie

For a Healthy Fat-Packed Avocado and Flaxseed Smoothie, blend together half an avocado, a spoonful of ground flaxseeds, a handful of spinach, a banana, and a cup of almond milk. This smoothie is high in healthy fats, which can support your body's detox processes.

Smoothies for Liver Detoxification

The liver plays a crucial role in the body's detoxification processes, and it's important to consume foods that support its health. Beets, for instance, are known for their liver-cleansing properties and can be included in your detox smoothies.

Recipe: Liver Cleansing Beet and Carrot Smoothie

To make a Liver Cleansing Beet and Carrot Smoothie, blend together one small beetroot, one carrot, an apple, a squeeze of lemon, and a cup of water. This smoothie is packed with liver-supporting ingredients, aiding your body's detox processes.

Avoiding Toxins in Your Detox Smoothies

While we're discussing detoxification, it's crucial to consider the potential sources of toxins in our diet. Many fruits and vegetables, especially those that are non-organic, can carry residues of pesticides, which can add to the body's toxin load. When making your detox smoothies, opt for organic produce whenever possible to limit your exposure to these potentially harmful chemicals.

Green Smoothie Revolution

Recipe: Organic Kale and Apple Detox Smoothie

For an Organic Kale and Apple Detox Smoothie, blend together a handful of organic kale, an organic apple, a slice of organic lemon, a teaspoon of organic chia seeds, and a cup of filtered water. The ingredients in this smoothie are all organic, reducing your exposure to pesticides and other potential toxins.

Herbs and Spices That Aid in Detoxification

Herbs and spices are not just flavor enhancers; many of them also have potent detoxification properties. For instance, cilantro has been shown to help remove heavy metals from the body, while ginger can aid in digestion and reduce inflammation.

Recipe: Cilantro and Ginger Detox Smoothie

To make a Cilantro and Ginger Detox Smoothie, blend together a handful of fresh cilantro, a small piece of fresh ginger, half a cucumber, a green apple, and a cup of coconut water. This smoothie is rich in detoxifying herbs and spices that can support your body's detox processes.

The Role of Citrus Fruits in Detoxification

Citrus fruits like lemons and oranges are high in vitamin C, a potent antioxidant that aids the body's natural detoxification processes. Additionally, these fruits can stimulate the liver's detox enzymes, further supporting detoxification.

Recipe: Citrus-Packed Orange and Lemon Smoothie

For a Citrus-Packed Orange and Lemon Smoothie, blend together one peeled orange, the juice of half a lemon, a banana, a handful of fresh spinach, and a cup of water. This smoothie is packed with vitamin C and other detoxifying nutrients, aiding in the body's detoxification processes.

Proper Timing and Regularity for Detox Smoothies

While incorporating detox smoothies into your diet can be beneficial, it's essential to also pay attention to timing and regularity. Consuming a detox smoothie sporadically might not yield the desired results. Instead, aim to include these nutrient-packed beverages in your regular routine for optimal benefits.

Recipe: Everyday Detox Green Smoothie

For an Everyday Detox Green Smoothie, blend together a handful of kale, a green apple, a small piece of fresh ginger, a tablespoon of chia seeds, and a cup of coconut water. This smoothie can be consumed daily to support your body's detoxification processes.

In Conclusion: Long-Term Detoxification Strategies

While the recipes and tips provided in this chapter can indeed aid in detoxification, it's important to remember that true detoxification is a long-term strategy and not a one-time event. Consistently making choices that support your body's detox processes, like eating a nutrient-dense diet, getting regular exercise, staying hydrated, and managing stress, are key to long-term detoxification success.

By incorporating these smoothie recipes into your regular routine and maintaining overall healthy habits, you can support your body's natural detox processes and work towards better health and wellness. Remember, it's always important to consult with a healthcare professional before making significant changes to your diet or lifestyle. Happy blending and detoxing!

Chapter 8

Building Immunity: Smoothies to Boost Your Defense System

Your immune system is your body's defense against illness and disease. It includes various organs, cells, and proteins that work together to fight off harmful substances like bacteria, viruses, and foreign bodies. A strong immune system is vital for maintaining overall health, and the foods you eat play a significant role in supporting it.

The Role of Vitamins and Minerals in Immune Health

Vitamins and minerals are critical for maintaining a healthy immune system. Some of the most crucial nutrients for immune health include vitamin C, vitamin D, vitamin E, vitamin A, zinc, selenium, and iron. Including smoothie ingredients rich in these nutrients can help support a healthy immune system.

Vitamin C-Rich Smoothies

Vitamin C is an essential nutrient for immune health. It aids in the production of white blood cells, which are crucial for fighting off infections. Citrus fruits like oranges, strawberries, kiwi, and pineapple are excellent sources of vitamin C.

Recipe: Vitamin C-Packed Citrus Smoothie

For a Vitamin C-Packed Citrus Smoothie, blend together one peeled orange, half a grapefruit, a handful of strawberries, and a cup of coconut water. This smoothie is loaded with vitamin C, supporting your immune health.

Green Smoothie Revolution

The Importance of Vitamin D in Immune Health

Vitamin D is another essential nutrient for immune health. It can modulate the immune responses and reduce inflammation. While our bodies can produce vitamin D when exposed to sunlight, many people do not get enough sun exposure, especially during the winter months. Including sources of vitamin D in your diet, like fortified dairy or non-dairy milk, can help ensure you're getting enough of this essential nutrient.

Recipe: Vitamin D-Rich Blueberry Almond Smoothie

For a Vitamin D-Rich Blueberry Almond Smoothie, blend together a cup of blueberries, a banana, a handful of almonds, and a cup of fortified almond milk. This smoothie provides a good source of vitamin D, along with other essential nutrients for immune health.

Zinc and Immune Health

Zinc is a mineral that's crucial for immune health. It aids in the production of immune cells and helps maintain the skin's integrity, the body's first line of defense against pathogens. Foods like pumpkin seeds, spinach, and mushrooms are good sources of zinc.

Recipe: Zinc-Packed Pumpkin Seed and Spinach Smoothie

For a Zinc-Packed Pumpkin Seed and Spinach Smoothie, blend together a handful of spinach, a banana, a quarter cup of pumpkin seeds, a cup of fortified almond milk, and a spoonful of honey. This smoothie is high in zinc, along with other nutrients that can support immune health.

Fiber and Gut Health

The health of your gut plays a significant role in the health of your immune system. The majority of your immune cells reside in your gut, and maintaining a healthy gut microbiota is essential for immune health. Fiber-rich ingredients like chia seeds, flax seeds, and fruits can help support a healthy gut, thereby supporting immune health.

Recipe: Fiber-Rich Chia Seed and Flaxseed Smoothie

For a Fiber-Rich Chia Seed and Flaxseed Smoothie, blend together a banana, a handful of spinach, a tablespoon of chia seeds, a tablespoon of ground flaxseeds, and a cup of almond milk. This smoothie is high in fiber, supporting your gut and immune health.

Probiotics and Gut Health

Probiotics are beneficial bacteria that can help maintain a healthy gut microbiota. They can be found in fermented foods like yogurt and kefir. Including probiotics in your smoothies can help support your gut and immune health.

Recipe: Probiotic-Packed Yogurt and Berry Smoothie

For a Probiotic-Packed Yogurt and Berry Smoothie, blend together a cup of mixed berries, a banana, a cup of yogurt, and a spoonful of honey. This smoothie is rich in probiotics, supporting your gut and immune health.

Recipe: Immune-Boosting Green Smoothie

Leafy greens are an excellent source of many of the vitamins and minerals necessary for a healthy immune system. In particular, they're high in vitamin C, vitamin K, and fiber. This immune-boosting green smoothie combines nutrient-dense leafy greens with other immune-supporting ingredients for a powerful health punch.

For this smoothie, you will need:

2 cups of spinach or kale
1 ripe banana
1/2 cup of pineapple
1 tablespoon of chia seeds
1 tablespoon of honey
1 cup of almond milk

Combine all ingredients in a blender and blend until smooth. This smoothie provides a healthy dose of vitamins C and K from the leafy greens, vitamin C and bromelain (a natural anti-inflammatory compound) from the pineapple, omega-3 fatty acids from the chia seeds, and additional nutrients from the banana and almond milk.

Green Smoothie Revolution

The Role of Healthy Fats in Immune Health

Dietary fats play an important role in immune function. Omega-3 fatty acids, in particular, are known for their anti-inflammatory properties and can help modulate immune responses. Foods high in omega-3 fatty acids include flax seeds, chia seeds, and walnuts.

Recipe: Omega-3 Powerhouse Smoothie

For a smoothie high in omega-3 fatty acids, you will need:

1 cup of spinach
1 ripe banana
1/2 cup of blueberries
1 tablespoon of flax seeds
1 tablespoon of chia seeds
1 tablespoon of walnuts
1 cup of almond milk
Combine all ingredients in a blender and blend until smooth. This smoothie provides a good source of omega-3 fatty acids from the flax seeds, chia seeds, and walnuts, along with a mix of vitamins and minerals from the other ingredients.

Hydration and Immune Health

Hydration plays a crucial role in overall health, including immune function. Water helps to carry oxygen to your body cells, which results in properly functioning systems. It also works in removing toxins from the body, thus cleansing it and making it less prone to disease.

Recipe: Hydrating Watermelon Smoothie

For a hydrating smoothie, try this watermelon smoothie recipe. Watermelon is not only hydrating but also high in vitamins A and C.

2 cups of watermelon
1 ripe banana
Juice of 1 lime
1 cup of coconut water

Combine all ingredients in a blender and blend until smooth. This smoothie is high in vitamins A and C from the watermelon, potassium from the banana, and electrolytes from the coconut water, making it an excellent choice for hydration.

Herbs and Spices for Immune Health

Certain herbs and spices have been recognized for their health-promoting properties, including immune support. Ginger, for example, is known for its anti-inflammatory and antioxidative effects, while turmeric contains curcumin, a compound with potent anti-inflammatory properties.

Recipe: Ginger-Turmeric Immune-Boosting Smoothie

For a smoothie that takes advantage of the immune-boosting properties of herbs and spices, try the following recipe:

1 ripe banana
1/2 cup of pineapple
1 tablespoon of fresh ginger
1 teaspoon of turmeric
1 cup of coconut milk

Combine all ingredients in a blender and blend until smooth. This smoothie contains anti-inflammatory compounds from the ginger and turmeric, vitamins C and bromelain from the pineapple, and healthy fats from the coconut milk.

Incorporating Smoothies Into a Healthy Lifestyle

Remember, while these smoothies can help support a healthy immune system, they should be part of a balanced diet that includes a variety of foods. Regular physical activity, adequate sleep, good hygiene practices, and avoiding harmful behaviors such as smoking and excessive alcohol consumption are also important for maintaining a healthy immune system.

Probiotics and Immune Health

Probiotics, the beneficial bacteria in your gut, play an essential role in the health of your immune system. They help to regulate immune responses and can protect against harmful bacteria that can cause illness. Fermented foods and yogurt are excellent sources of probiotics.

Recipe: Probiotic-Rich Berry Yogurt Smoothie

A delicious way to incorporate more probiotics into your diet is with a probiotic-rich smoothie. Here's a recipe:

1 cup of mixed berries (like strawberries, blueberries, and raspberries)
1 ripe banana
1 cup of Greek yogurt
1 tablespoon of honey
1/2 cup of almond milk
Combine all ingredients in a blender and blend until smooth. The Greek yogurt provides beneficial probiotics, while the berries offer a good source of vitamins and antioxidants.

Vitamin D and Immune Health

Vitamin D is another important nutrient for immune health. It plays a role in the activation of immune system defenses, and a deficiency in vitamin D can lead to increased susceptibility to infection.

Recipe: Sunshine Smoothie

For a smoothie that's high in vitamin D, try this recipe:

1 ripe banana
1/2 cup of orange juice
1/2 cup of Greek yogurt
1 tablespoon of honey
1/2 cup of almond milk
Combine all ingredients in a blender and blend until smooth. The Greek yogurt and almond milk provide a good source of vitamin D, while the orange juice offers a healthy dose of vitamin C.

Zinc and Immune Health

Zinc is an essential mineral that plays a significant role in the immune system. It helps to regulate immune responses and has been found to be crucial for the development and function of immune cells.

Recipe: Zinc-Boosting Pumpkin Seed Smoothie

Pumpkin seeds are an excellent source of zinc. Incorporate them into your smoothies for an added nutritional punch. Here's a recipe to get you started:

1 ripe banana
1 tablespoon of pumpkin seeds
1 cup of spinach
1 tablespoon of honey
1 cup of almond milk

Combine all ingredients in a blender and blend until smooth. This smoothie provides a good source of zinc from the pumpkin seeds, as well as a host of vitamins and minerals from the other ingredients.

Balancing Nutrients in Smoothies

While it's essential to focus on incorporating certain nutrients into your smoothies, it's equally important to create balanced smoothies that provide a variety of nutrients. A well-balanced smoothie includes a source of protein (such as yogurt or protein powder), fruits and/or vegetables for vitamins and minerals, a healthy fat (like nuts, seeds, or avocado), and a liquid (such as milk, water, or juice).

Remember to enjoy these smoothies as part of a balanced diet. Incorporate a variety of ingredients to get the widest range of nutrients and avoid relying solely on smoothies for nutrition. A healthy diet includes a variety of foods from all food groups, and smoothies are an excellent way to supplement your nutrient intake, not replace meals.

In conclusion, smoothies are a versatile and delicious way to support your immune system and overall health. By carefully selecting ingredients that offer immune-boosting nutrients, you can create a powerful beverage that not only tastes good but also supports your body's defenses. Enjoy exploring different combinations of ingredients and flavors, and boost your health one smoothie at a time!

Chapter 9

Kids' Corner: Kid-Friendly Smoothies Even the Pickiest Eater Will Love

Getting kids to eat a balanced diet can be a challenge, especially when it comes to fruits and vegetables. Smoothies can be a fantastic solution. They're a fun, kid-friendly way to pack a variety of nutrients into a single glass. In this chapter, we'll dive into the benefits of smoothies for children, and tips on how to make smoothies appeal to the little ones. We'll also share a variety of kid-approved smoothie recipes that even the pickiest eater will love.

Smoothies and Kids: A Perfect Pair

Smoothies and kids are a perfect pair. Kids love the sweet taste and vibrant colors of smoothies, and parents love the fact that they're an easy way to get fruits, vegetables, and other essential nutrients into their child's diet. Smoothies can be a valuable tool in promoting healthier eating habits, serving as a nutritious alternative to sugary drinks, and providing energy for active kids.

Making Smoothies Kid-Friendly

The key to making smoothies kid-friendly is to focus on taste and presentation. Kids are more likely to enjoy a smoothie if it tastes good and looks appealing. Here are some tips:

Start with fruits they love: If your child is new to smoothies, start with fruits they already enjoy. As they get used to the idea of drinking their fruits and vegetables, you can gradually introduce new flavors and ingredients.

Green Smoothie Revolution

Add natural sweetness: If your child finds some smoothies too bitter or sour, consider adding a natural sweetener like honey, agave nectar, or a ripe banana.

Get creative with colors: Kids are drawn to vibrant colors, so use a mix of fruits and vegetables to create colorful smoothies. Think bright green smoothies with spinach and pineapple, or beautiful purple smoothies with mixed berries.

Involve them in the process: Let your child be part of the smoothie-making process. They can help choose the ingredients, add them to the blender, and even press the blend button. This will make them more interested in trying the final product.

Kid-Friendly Smoothie Recipes

Now, let's get to the fun part – making smoothies that your kids will love! Here are several kid-approved smoothie recipes to get you started.

1. Banana and Strawberry Smoothie

A classic combination that kids love, bananas and strawberries come together to create a deliciously creamy and sweet smoothie.

Ingredients:

1 ripe banana
1 cup of strawberries
1 cup of almond milk
1 tablespoon of honey
Instructions:

Combine all ingredients in a blender and blend until smooth. Serve immediately.

2. Mango Pineapple Smoothie

The tropical flavors of mango and pineapple make for a refreshingly sweet smoothie that kids will love.

Ingredients:

1 cup of mango chunks
1 cup of pineapple chunks
1 cup of coconut milk
1 tablespoon of honey
Instructions:

Combine all ingredients in a blender and blend until smooth. Serve immediately.

3. Peanut Butter Banana Smoothie

The addition of peanut butter adds a delicious nutty flavor that kids enjoy, and the banana provides natural sweetness.

Ingredients:

1 ripe banana
1 cup of almond milk
1 tablespoon of natural peanut butter
1 tablespoon of honey
Instructions:

Combine all ingredients in a blender and blend until smooth. Serve immediately.

4. Green Monster Smoothie

Don't let the color fool you – this green smoothie tastes delicious and is packed with nutrients. The addition of a ripe banana and a hint of honey helps to balance out the taste of the spinach, making it kid-friendly.

Ingredients:

1 ripe banana
1 cup of fresh spinach
1 cup of almond milk
1 tablespoon of honey

Instructions:

Combine all ingredients in a blender and blend until smooth. Serve immediately.

5. Chocolate Avocado Smoothie

This smoothie combines the creaminess of avocado with the rich flavor of cocoa powder. The result is a deliciously smooth and chocolatey smoothie that kids won't be able to resist.

Ingredients:

1 ripe banana
1/2 ripe avocado
1 tablespoon of unsweetened cocoa powder
1 cup of almond milk
1 tablespoon of honey
Instructions:

Combine all ingredients in a blender and blend until smooth. Serve immediately.
Introducing Smoothies to Picky Eaters

Introducing new foods to picky eaters can be a daunting task. But with smoothies, it doesn't have to be. Smoothies provide an excellent way to sneak in fruits, vegetables, and other nutrient-rich foods that your child might otherwise refuse to eat. Here are a few tips:

Start Small: If your child is very picky, you can begin by adding a small amount of a new ingredient to a smoothie recipe that they already enjoy. For instance, you can add a handful of spinach to a strawberry banana smoothie. They might not even notice it!

Balance Flavors: Make sure to balance the flavors. If you're adding vegetables, make sure there's enough fruit to mask the taste. A ripe banana or some honey can sweeten a smoothie without resorting to refined sugar.

Experiment with Textures: Some kids are sensitive to textures. If your child doesn't like chunky smoothies, make sure to blend the smoothie thoroughly until it's perfectly smooth. Conversely, if your child likes a bit of chew, add some unblended nuts or granola on top.

Picky-Eater Approved Smoothie Recipes

The following recipes are designed with picky eaters in mind. They are sweet, visually appealing, and packed with hidden nutrients.

1. Hidden Veggie Blueberry Smoothie

This smoothie is a great way to sneak in some vegetables. The blueberries give it a vibrant color, masking the fact that it contains spinach!

Ingredients:

1 cup of blueberries
1 ripe banana
1 handful of spinach
1 cup of Greek yogurt
1 tablespoon of honey
Instructions:

Combine all ingredients in a blender and blend until smooth. Serve immediately.

2. Creamy Peanut Butter and Jelly Smoothie

This smoothie mimics the taste of a peanut butter and jelly sandwich, a childhood favorite. The berries give it a sweetness and a vibrant color, while the peanut butter adds a comforting, familiar flavor.

Ingredients:

1 cup of mixed berries
1 ripe banana
2 tablespoons of natural peanut butter
1 cup of almond milk

Green Smoothie Revolution

Instructions:

Combine all ingredients in a blender and blend until smooth. Serve immediately.

3. Sweet Carrot Cake Smoothie

This smoothie is inspired by the flavors of a carrot cake. The sweetness of the pineapple and the banana balances the taste of the carrot. The addition of the Greek yogurt gives it a rich, creamy texture that's reminiscent of a cake batter.

Ingredients:

1 cup of chopped carrots
1 ripe banana
1 cup of chopped pineapple
1 cup of Greek yogurt
1 teaspoon of cinnamon
Instructions:

Combine all ingredients in a blender and blend until smooth. Serve immediately.

4. Tropical Green Monster Smoothie

Don't be fooled by its green color; this smoothie tastes like a tropical paradise. The pineapple and the mango give it a tropical flavor, and the spinach is barely noticeable.

Ingredients:

1 cup of fresh spinach
1 cup of chopped mango
1 cup of chopped pineapple
1 ripe banana
1 cup of coconut milk
Instructions:

Combine all ingredients in a blender and blend until smooth. Serve immediately.

Smoothies offer an easy, delicious way to introduce a variety of fruits and vegetables into your child's diet. With a bit of creativity, you can create smoothies that not only taste great but are also packed with essential nutrients.
Fun and Interactive Smoothie Making

Another excellent way to get children interested in smoothies is to make the process fun and interactive. Getting your kids involved in the smoothie-making process can pique their interest and make them more likely to try new things. Here's how:

Let Them Choose: Allow your children to choose some of the ingredients for the smoothie. For example, they can pick the fruits and the color of the smoothie. This gives them a sense of control over their food, which can be very motivating.

Fun Shapes and Colors: Use cookie cutters to cut fruits into fun shapes for garnishing the smoothie. Similarly, using ingredients of different colors can make the smoothie more visually appealing. For example, a rainbow smoothie with layers of different colored fruits can be an exciting project.

Taste Test: Let your kids taste the smoothie at different stages of the process. This will make them feel involved and excited about the final product.

Interactive Smoothie Recipes

1. Rainbow Layered Smoothie

This smoothie is a feast for the eyes and the taste buds. Each layer represents a different color of the rainbow, making this a fun and healthy project that your kids will love.

Ingredients:

Red layer: 1 cup strawberries, 1 banana

Green Smoothie Revolution

Orange layer: 1 cup peaches, 1 orange
Yellow layer: 1 cup pineapple, 1 banana
Green layer: 1 cup spinach, 1 green apple
Blue layer: 1 cup blueberries, 1 banana
Purple layer: 1 cup mixed berries, 1 banana
1-2 cups of milk (can be dairy or non-dairy), divided
Instructions:

For each layer, blend the fruit with a bit of milk until smooth, rinse the blender between each layer, and pour into a glass, freezing for a few minutes between each layer to keep them separate. Repeat with all colors and serve with a straw and a spoon to enjoy each layer separately or mix them together.

2. Monster Green Smoothie

The name and vibrant color of this smoothie make it a fun choice for kids. Despite its name, it tastes sweet and fruity.

Ingredients:

1 cup of fresh spinach
1 cup of pineapple chunks
1 ripe banana
1/2 cup of Greek yogurt
1/2 cup of orange juice
A few slices of kiwi for garnishing
Instructions:

Blend the spinach, pineapple, banana, yogurt, and orange juice until smooth. Pour into a glass, garnish with kiwi slices to make "monster eyes," and serve with a colorful straw.

3. Chocolate Peanut Butter Banana Smoothie

This smoothie tastes like a dessert but is filled with nutritious ingredients. It's a win-win for both parents and kids.

Ingredients:

2 ripe bananas
2 tablespoons of natural peanut butter
1 tablespoon of cocoa powder
1 cup of Greek yogurt
1/2 cup of milk
A few chocolate chips for garnishing
Instructions:

Blend the bananas, peanut butter, cocoa powder, Greek yogurt, and milk until smooth. Pour into a glass, garnish with a few chocolate chips, and serve with a straw.

Involving your kids in the smoothie-making process not only makes it more fun but also provides an opportunity for them to learn about different fruits, vegetables, and their nutritional benefits.
Incorporating Smoothies into Kid-Friendly Meals

Smoothies don't always have to be a standalone treat - they can easily be incorporated into meals, especially breakfast. You can make a more substantial meal by pairing a smoothie with other kid-friendly foods. Here are a few ideas:

1. Smoothie and Pancakes

Who doesn't love pancakes? You can make this breakfast even more nutritious by serving it with a fruit smoothie instead of the usual sugary syrup. For example, a banana and blueberry smoothie can be a delicious, healthy substitute for syrup.

2. Smoothie and Sandwich

A sandwich filled with their favorite ingredients, like cheese or peanut butter, and a glass of smoothie can make a balanced lunch. The sandwich provides proteins and carbs, while the smoothie adds a serving of fruits and/or vegetables.

3. Smoothie and Cereal

A bowl of cereal with milk, topped with some fresh fruits, and a side of a refreshing smoothie can be a great way to start the day. Choose cereals that are low in sugar and high in fiber to ensure that the meal is healthy.

4. Smoothie Popsicles

Smoothie popsicles are a great way to serve smoothies, especially during the summer. Pour any of your favorite smoothie recipes into popsicle molds and freeze them for a few hours. They make a perfect dessert or snack.

Remember, the goal is to pair the smoothie with foods that complement its nutritional profile. That way, your child gets a balanced intake of proteins, carbohydrates, and fruits/vegetables.

Addressing Common Objections

While smoothies can be a great way to introduce kids to fruits and vegetables, it's not uncommon to face some resistance. Here are a few common objections kids might have and ways to address them:

"I don't like the color."
Some children might be put off by green smoothies or smoothies in colors they don't find appealing. In such cases, use fruits like strawberries, raspberries, or blueberries to change the color. Or, serve the smoothie in a colorful cup with a lid and a fun straw, so the color of the smoothie isn't visible.

"It tastes weird."
If your child doesn't like the taste of a smoothie, try to figure out what they don't like about it. If it's too bitter, add a bit more fruit or a spoonful of honey. If it's the taste of a specific fruit or vegetable they don't like, try replacing it with something else.

"I don't like the texture."
The texture of a smoothie can be a big factor for some children. If they find it too thick, add some more liquid to thin it out. If they don't like the bits of fruits or veggies, try blending the smoothie longer until it's smoother.
Sneaky Smoothies: Incorporating Veggies into Kids' Smoothies

While fruit smoothies are usually a hit with kids, vegetable-based smoothies might not be as welcomed. The great news is that there are plenty of ways to sneak in those vegetables without the kiddos even noticing. The key is choosing vegetables with neutral or sweet flavors and balancing them with the sweetness of the fruit.

1. Spinach and Kale

These green leafy vegetables are packed with nutrients but can be a bit hard to sell to a child due to their distinct taste. The trick here is to balance out the flavor with sweet fruits like bananas, mangoes, or peaches. Starting with a small amount and gradually increasing it as they get used to the taste can also be helpful.

2. Carrots

Carrots have a naturally sweet flavor, making them an excellent addition to smoothies. They pair well with oranges, mangoes, and bananas. Plus, they add a beautiful orange color to the smoothie, which kids love.

3. Avocado

Avocado adds creaminess to the smoothie, which can make it more appealing to kids. Its mild flavor can be easily masked with fruits like strawberries or bananas. Avocado is also packed with healthy fats, which are great for children's development.

4. Zucchini

Zucchini is another vegetable with a neutral flavor that can be easily added to smoothies. It's great in combination with pineapple, apple, or berries. Just make sure to peel it first to avoid adding any green color to the smoothie.

5. Sweet Potato

Cooked sweet potato can make a smoothie taste like dessert. It pairs well with cinnamon and nutmeg for a pumpkin pie-like flavor. Sweet potatoes are packed with vitamin A and fiber, making them a great addition to your child's diet.

Creating a Routine: Smoothie Challenges and Rewards

Creating a fun smoothie routine can also make kids more excited about their daily glass of nutrients. You can do this by setting up smoothie challenges, where they get to create their own smoothie recipes, or by rewarding them for trying out new vegetables in their smoothies.

A fun idea is to create a "smoothie calendar" where you plan different smoothie recipes for each day of the week. You can involve your children in the planning process, letting them choose some of the ingredients. This can be a great way to teach them about different fruits and vegetables and their nutritional benefits.

In conclusion, making kid-friendly smoothies is all about creativity and balance. By using fruits to mask the flavor of vegetables, introducing new ingredients gradually, and making the whole process fun, you can help your kids develop healthy eating habits that will last a lifetime. Remember, the goal isn't to trick them into eating vegetables but rather to help them learn to enjoy them in a fun and tasty way.

Chapter 10

Smoothies for Special Diets: Vegan, Keto, and Gluten-Free Recipes

The beauty of smoothies lies in their versatility. Not only can they cater to your taste buds, but they can also be adapted to meet various dietary requirements. This chapter is dedicated to providing delicious and nutritious smoothie recipes for those on special diets. It will cover vegan, keto, and gluten-free diets, offering a rich blend of recipes that will ensure everyone gets a piece of the smoothie delight.

Vegan Smoothies

Adopting a vegan diet involves eliminating all animal-derived ingredients. This might sound challenging when it comes to smoothies, given that popular additions such as yogurt or whey protein aren't allowed. However, there are plenty of plant-based alternatives that can yield equally delectable and healthy vegan smoothies.

Substitutes for dairy: Instead of milk or yogurt, opt for plant-based alternatives such as almond milk, coconut milk, oat milk, or soy milk. They are creamy and can add a nice flavor to your smoothie.

Protein sources: It's crucial to incorporate protein into your vegan smoothies, especially if they're serving as a meal replacement. Vegan protein sources can include tofu, chia seeds, hemp seeds, and plant-based protein powders.

Healthy fats: Avocados, chia seeds, flaxseeds, and nuts are excellent sources of healthy fats that can make your smoothies more satiating.

Keto Smoothies

The ketogenic, or keto, diet is a low-carb, high-fat diet. The goal is to get your body into a state of ketosis, where it burns fat for fuel instead of carbohydrates. Making a keto-friendly smoothie can be a bit tricky because many fruits are high in carbs and thus avoided on a keto diet.

Low-carb fruits: Berries, such as strawberries, blueberries, and raspberries, are lower in carbs than most fruits and can be included in your keto smoothies in moderate amounts.

Healthy fats: As the keto diet is high in fats, adding ingredients like avocados, nut butter, or coconut cream can help increase the fat content of your smoothies.

Protein sources: Whey or casein protein powders are generally keto-friendly. However, check the labels to ensure they don't have added sugars. You can also add full-fat Greek yogurt for a protein boost.

Gluten-Free Smoothies

For those with celiac disease or non-celiac gluten sensitivity, finding gluten-free foods can be a challenge. Fortunately, smoothies are naturally gluten-free, as long as you pay attention to some details.

Fruits and vegetables: Most fruits and vegetables are naturally gluten-free and are excellent bases for your smoothies.

Liquids: Use milk or plant-based milks like almond milk or coconut milk. Be careful with oat milk, as not all oats are gluten-free.

Protein sources: Protein powders can sometimes contain gluten, so it's crucial to read labels carefully. Opt for powders labeled gluten-free to be safe.

Add-ins: Chia seeds, flaxseeds, nuts, and spices are all great gluten-free add-ins. Avoid malt-based products, as malt contains gluten.
Creating Vegan Smoothies

Creating vegan smoothies is a process that can be fun and experimental, as there are countless combinations of fruits, vegetables, and vegan-friendly ingredients that you can mix and match. Let's delve into some tips and a few delicious vegan smoothie recipes:

Opt for unsweetened plant milks: Unsweetened almond or soy milk can be an excellent base for vegan smoothies as they don't contain added sugars.

Add some veggies: Don't shy away from adding vegetables to your smoothies. Spinach, kale, and cucumbers blend well with fruits and offer additional nutrients.

Freeze your fruits: Using frozen fruits not only makes your smoothie chill and refreshing but also provides a thicker texture.

Recipes

Creamy Vegan Strawberry Banana Smoothie
Ingredients:

1 cup of unsweetened almond milk
1 ripe banana (preferably frozen)
1 cup of strawberries (fresh or frozen)
1 tablespoon of chia seeds
A handful of spinach
Blend all ingredients in a high-speed blender until smooth and creamy. Enjoy immediately for the best taste.

Green Goddess Smoothie
Ingredients:

1 cup of unsweetened almond milk
1 ripe banana
1 cup of fresh spinach
1 tablespoon of chia seeds
1 tablespoon of almond butter
Blend all ingredients together until smooth. Enjoy immediately, garnishing with some almond flakes if desired.

Designing Keto Smoothies

Mendocino Brock

While the idea of a low-carb smoothie might seem challenging at first, the key to designing keto smoothies is choosing the right low-carb ingredients and being creative with your combinations.

Choose low-carb fruits: Berries, such as strawberries, raspberries, and blackberries, are relatively low in carbs and can provide the sweetness you desire in your smoothie.

Incorporate high-fat ingredients: Since the keto diet is high in fats, consider adding ingredients like avocados or a spoonful of MCT oil or coconut oil to increase the fat content.

Use unsweetened plant milk or water as a base: Milk contains lactose, a type of sugar. So it's better to opt for unsweetened almond milk or even just water for your keto smoothie base.

Recipes

Keto Berry Bliss Smoothie
Ingredients:

1 cup of unsweetened almond milk
1/2 cup of mixed berries (fresh or frozen)
1 tablespoon of MCT oil or coconut oil
1 scoop of low-carb protein powder (optional)
Blend all ingredients together until smooth. If the smoothie is too thick, you can add a little more almond milk or water until it reaches your desired consistency.

Creamy Avocado Keto Smoothie
Ingredients:

1 cup of unsweetened almond milk
1/2 ripe avocado
1/2 cup of spinach
1 tablespoon of MCT oil or coconut oil
1 scoop of low-carb protein powder (optional)
A few ice cubes

Green Smoothie Revolution

Blend all ingredients until smooth. This creamy smoothie is not only low in carbs but also high in healthy fats, making it a perfect breakfast or snack for the keto diet.

Creating Gluten-Free Smoothies

For those following a gluten-free diet, the great news is that most smoothies are naturally gluten-free. However, be cautious with store-bought smoothies or smoothie mixes as they might contain additives that contain gluten. When making your own gluten-free smoothies, the possibilities are endless.

Tips for Gluten-Free Smoothies

Whole Foods: Use whole fruits and vegetables in your smoothies, as they are naturally gluten-free.

Add Ins: For extra protein, fiber, and nutrition, add in seeds like chia, flax, or hemp. These are all gluten-free and add extra nutrients and texture to your smoothies.

Non-Dairy Milks: Most non-dairy milks are gluten-free, but always check the labels to be sure there are no additives that contain gluten.

Recipes

Blueberry Muffin Smoothie
Ingredients:

1 cup of unsweetened almond milk
1 ripe banana (preferably frozen)
1 cup of fresh or frozen blueberries
1 tablespoon of chia seeds
1 tablespoon of almond butter
Blend all ingredients in a high-speed blender until smooth. The result is a smoothie that tastes like a blueberry muffin but is packed with nutrients and is gluten-free.

Chocolate Avocado Smoothie
Ingredients:

1 cup of unsweetened almond milk
1 ripe banana
1 ripe avocado
2 tablespoons of unsweetened cocoa powder
1 tablespoon of honey or maple syrup
Blend all ingredients together until smooth. This smoothie is like a dessert in a glass, yet it's packed with healthy fats from the avocado and is gluten-free.

Smoothies are not only a quick and easy way to get more fruits and vegetables in your diet, but they can also be tailored to fit any dietary needs or preferences. Whether you're vegan, on a keto diet, or following a gluten-free diet, you can enjoy the benefits and versatility of smoothies.
Paleo-Friendly Smoothies

For individuals following a paleo diet, smoothies are a fantastic option because they offer an easy way to incorporate a variety of fruits and vegetables into your diet. However, since the paleo diet excludes grains, dairy, and refined sugars, you'll need to be careful about your ingredient selection. Here are some tips:

Fruits and Vegetables: Any fruit or vegetable is a great choice, but opt for those lower in sugar like berries or green leafy vegetables.

Protein: Add a scoop of paleo-friendly protein powder or collagen peptides for an extra boost.

Non-Dairy Milk: Almond milk, coconut milk, and other non-dairy milks are excellent for paleo smoothies.

Sweeteners: Opt for natural sweeteners like raw honey or dates, but use them sparingly due to their sugar content.

Recipes

Green Machine Paleo Smoothie
Ingredients:

1 cup of unsweetened almond milk
1 ripe banana

2 cups of spinach
1 tablespoon of almond butter
1 tablespoon of chia seeds
Blend all ingredients in a high-speed blender until smooth. This nutrient-packed green smoothie is perfect for a quick breakfast or snack.

Paleo Berry Blast
Ingredients:

1 cup of unsweetened coconut milk
1 cup of mixed berries
1 ripe banana
1 tablespoon of raw honey
1 scoop of paleo-friendly protein powder
Blend all ingredients until smooth. This smoothie is bursting with antioxidants from the berries and has an added protein boost.

In essence, whether you're following a specific diet due to allergies, health concerns, or personal choices, you can still enjoy a wide range of delicious and nutritious smoothies. From vegan to keto to gluten-free and beyond, there's a smoothie out there for everyone. And remember, these recipes are just a starting point - feel free to get creative and make these smoothies your own.

125

Chapter 11

The Art of Smoothie-Making: Tips and Tricks for the Perfect Blend

Becoming a smoothie master requires more than just tossing ingredients into a blender and hoping for the best. Like any culinary endeavor, creating the perfect smoothie requires a little knowledge, practice, and a dash of creativity. In this chapter, we'll delve into the art of smoothie-making, offering tips and tricks to help you achieve the perfect blend every time.

Understanding Your Blender

Your blender is your most crucial tool in smoothie making. Understanding how to use it effectively can significantly impact the quality of your smoothies. Here are some points to consider:

Blender Speed: Start on a low speed to break up big pieces, then gradually increase the speed. Ending on a high speed can ensure a smoother blend.

Blender Cleanliness: After each use, it's vital to clean your blender properly. Leftover residue can affect the taste of your next smoothie and lead to bacterial growth.

Layering Ingredients

How you layer your ingredients can also affect the smoothie's texture and blending efficiency:

Liquids First: Adding your liquid base first will help your blender run smoothly and prevent ingredient buildup.

Soft Foods Next: After your liquid, add soft ingredients like leafy greens, bananas, or yogurt. This order helps create a vortex that pulls down the harder ingredients from the top.

Hard Ingredients Last: Hard and frozen items should be added last. They get pulled into the mix gradually, allowing your blender to work more efficiently.

Temperature and Consistency

How cold you want your smoothie and how thick you want it to be are personal preferences that you'll come to understand with experience:

Using Frozen Ingredients: Frozen ingredients can make your smoothie chillier and thicker. If your smoothie isn't cold enough, you can add ice, but do so sparingly to avoid watering it down.

Adjusting Consistency: If your smoothie is too thick, add more liquid. If it's too thin, add more fruit, vegetables, or ice.

Getting the Right Flavor

Creating a tasty smoothie is all about balancing the right flavors:

Sweetness: If your smoothie isn't sweet enough, consider adding a sweet fruit like banana or mango, a sweetener like honey or maple syrup, or a flavored yogurt.

Acidity: Citrus fruits like oranges or lemons can cut through the sweetness and add a refreshing tang.

Bitterness: If your smoothie is too bitter, this could be due to certain vegetables like kale or a high concentration of seeds. Counteract this by adding more sweet fruits or a sweetener.

Additional Tips

Green Smoothie Revolution

To Boost Nutrition: To give your smoothie an extra health kick, consider add-ins such as chia seeds, flax seeds, oats, protein powder, spirulina, or various nut butters.

To Enhance Flavor: To make your smoothie more flavorful, try adding natural flavors like vanilla or almond extract, spices like cinnamon or nutmeg, or fresh herbs like mint or basil.

Prep in Advance: If you're short on time in the morning, you can prep your smoothie the night before. Another option is to prepare smoothie packs to store in the freezer.

Smoothie Bowl: If you prefer to eat your smoothie with a spoon, make it thicker by reducing the liquid and topping it with fruits, nuts, seeds, or granola.

Experiment: Don't be afraid to experiment with different combinations of ingredients. You might discover your new favorite smoothie recipe in the process.

Balancing Nutritional Content

Creating a healthy smoothie is all about balance. Including a variety of ingredients will help you consume a wide range of nutrients. However, be mindful of the total caloric content. While smoothies are generally healthy, they can quickly become high in calories if you're not careful.

Protein: This is crucial for tissue repair and growth. You can incorporate protein in your smoothies through Greek yogurt, milk (dairy or non-dairy alternatives like soy or almond milk), protein powders, and nut butter.

Fiber: This helps with digestion and keeps you feeling full. Ingredients high in fiber include fruits, vegetables, oats, chia seeds, and flax seeds.

Healthy Fats: These are essential for absorbing certain vitamins and keeping you satiated. Avocados, chia seeds, flax seeds, and nut butters are excellent sources of healthy fats.

Carbohydrates: These provide energy. Fruits and vegetables are good sources of healthy carbs.

Vitamins & Minerals: To get a wide range of these, include different fruits, vegetables, and even some fortified dairy or non-dairy milk.

Creativity in Smoothie Making

There is no one-size-fits-all recipe in smoothie making. Don't be afraid to try out new combinations. Here are a few ideas:

Herbs and Spices: Adding fresh herbs and spices can give a unique flavor to your smoothie. Try mint, basil, cinnamon, ginger, or turmeric.

Tea: You can use cooled tea as a liquid base for added antioxidants and flavor. Green tea, chamomile, and hibiscus are great options.

Coffee: A splash of coffee can turn your smoothie into an energizing breakfast. Just be careful not to overdo it, especially if you're sensitive to caffeine.

Avocado: This fruit adds creaminess to your smoothie and is an excellent source of healthy fats and fiber.

The Role of Texture in Your Smoothies

The texture of your smoothie can greatly affect your enjoyment of it. Some people prefer a thinner, more drinkable smoothie, while others enjoy a thicker, spoonable consistency like a smoothie bowl. You can control the texture of your smoothie through the ratio of solid to liquid ingredients and whether or not you use frozen ingredients.

For a Thinner Smoothie: Use more liquid and fewer solid ingredients. Fresh fruits instead of frozen will also result in a thinner consistency.

For a Thicker Smoothie: Use less liquid and more solid ingredients. Frozen fruits or adding ingredients like yogurt, avocado, or ice can also make your smoothie thicker.

Experimenting with Color

Green Smoothie Revolution

We eat with our eyes first, and smoothies are no exception. The color of your smoothie can make it more appealing. Mix and match ingredients to create a range of colors:

Green: Spinach, kale, avocado, green apples, kiwi.

Red/Pink: Strawberries, raspberries, red apples, beets.

Purple/Blue: Blueberries, blackberries, purple grapes.

Orange/Yellow: Oranges, peaches, mangoes, carrots, pumpkin.

Brown: Don't be put off by the color! These smoothies often contain a mix of colorful fruits and vegetables, along with cocoa or protein powders.

Understanding the Importance of a Good Blender

Your blender is the most critical tool in smoothie-making, and understanding how to use it effectively can significantly impact the quality of your smoothies.

Power: A blender with a robust motor can crush ice and frozen fruits more easily, creating a smoother texture.

Blade Design: Blenders with multiple blade levels can help chop and combine the ingredients more evenly.

Settings: Many blenders have pre-programmed settings for different tasks, such as crushing ice or pureeing. Use these settings to your advantage.

Maintenance: A well-maintained blender lasts longer and performs better. Always clean your blender thoroughly after each use to prevent buildup and blade dulling.

Layering Ingredients for Optimal Blending

How you layer your ingredients in the blender can affect how well they blend together.

Liquids First: Start by adding your liquids. This helps the blender blades move freely.

Powders and Small Items Next: After the liquids, add any powders (like protein powder or cocoa), as well as small items like seeds or nuts. This helps to ensure that they get fully incorporated into the smoothie.

Soft Foods Then Hard Foods: Add soft foods, like fresh fruits, before hard foods, like frozen fruits or ice. This helps the blender process the harder items more efficiently.

Greens Last: Leafy greens should go on top. This helps them to get drawn into the blender more effectively, ensuring that they get fully blended.

Tips and Tricks for the Perfect Blend

Here are some additional tips to help you create the perfect smoothie:

Prep Ahead: If you're short on time in the mornings, prep your smoothie ingredients the night before. You can even pre-portion your ingredients and freeze them in individual servings for convenience.

Ice vs. Frozen Fruit: While ice can make your smoothie cold and frothy, too much can water it down. Using frozen fruit can help create a cold, thick smoothie without watering it down.

Don't Overblend: Over-blending can lead to a runny smoothie and can cause ingredients like seeds and nuts to become too finely processed.

Adjust to Taste: If your smoothie is too thick, add a little more liquid. If it's too thin, add more fruit or ice. If it's not sweet enough, add a touch of honey or a ripe banana. Remember, the perfect smoothie is one that tastes perfect to you!

Clean Immediately: Rinse your blender as soon as you're done making your smoothie. It's much easier to clean before the residue dries.

Going Beyond the Basics: Advanced Smoothie Techniques

Once you have mastered the basics of smoothie making, you can start to explore more advanced techniques that can bring your smoothies to the next level. Let's delve into a few of these techniques:

Incorporating Whole Grains and Seeds

You might be surprised to learn that whole grains and seeds can be added to smoothies, providing a source of complex carbohydrates, fiber, and a variety of other nutrients. Here are some examples:

Oats: Rolled oats or instant oats can be added to smoothies to provide a thicker texture and an added boost of fiber. It's best to soak them in your liquid base for a few minutes before blending to make them easier to blend.

Chia Seeds: These tiny seeds are packed with fiber, protein, and omega-3 fatty acids. They can be added directly to the smoothie or soaked beforehand to create a gel-like texture.

Flaxseeds: Flaxseeds are a great source of omega-3 fatty acids and fiber. Ground flaxseeds are easier to digest and can be blended directly into the smoothie.

Utilizing Natural Sweeteners

While fruit provides natural sweetness to your smoothies, sometimes you might want a little extra sweetness, especially in green or vegetable-based smoothies. Here are some natural sweeteners you can use:

Honey: Honey is a natural sweetener that also offers some health benefits, including antibacterial properties.

Maple Syrup: Maple syrup is another natural sweetener option that can add a unique flavor to your smoothies. Look for pure maple syrup, not pancake syrup, which can contain added sugars.

Dates: Dates are a whole food sweetener that provides not only sweetness but also fiber and nutrients. Just be sure to remove the pits before adding them to your blender!

Adding Healthy Fats

Healthy fats can help make your smoothies more satisfying and also help your body absorb fat-soluble vitamins. Here are some options:

Avocado: Adding half an avocado to your smoothie can create an incredibly creamy texture while also providing heart-healthy monounsaturated fats.

Nut Butters: Almond butter, peanut butter, or other nut butters can add both protein and healthy fats to your smoothies.

Coconut Milk: Full-fat coconut milk can add a tropical flavor to your smoothies along with a dose of healthy fats.

Customizing Your Smoothie's Nutritional Profile

Depending on your personal health goals or dietary needs, there might be additional ingredients you want to consider adding to your smoothies:

Protein Powder: If you're looking to increase your protein intake, a scoop of protein powder can be a great addition to your smoothies. There are many types available, including whey, soy, pea, and other plant-based options.

Greens Powder: If you're having trouble fitting enough vegetables into your day, consider adding a scoop of greens powder to your smoothie. These powders typically contain a variety of dehydrated and powdered vegetables, grasses, herbs, and other green foods.

Supplements: Depending on your health needs, you might also consider adding other supplements to your smoothies, like collagen for skin and joint health, probiotics for gut health, or specific vitamins and minerals.

The beauty of smoothie making is that there are endless possibilities. With these advanced techniques, you can experiment and create your own unique smoothie recipes that not only taste great but also meet your nutritional needs. Happy blending!

9 789493 212381